EMOTIONAL MATURITY
in LOVE and MARRIAGE

Books by Lucy Freeman

FIGHT AGAINST FEARS

HOPE FOR THE TROUBLED

BEFORE I KILL MORE

HOSPITAL IN ACTION

SEARCH FOR LOVE

SO YOU WANT TO BE PSYCHOANALYZED!

TROUBLED WOMEN

THE STORY OF PSYCHOANALYSIS (*written with Marvin Small*)

Books by Harold Greenwald

THE CALL GIRL: A PSYCHOANALYTICAL STUDY

GREAT CASES IN PSYCHOANALYSIS, *Editor*

LUCY FREEMAN AND HAROLD GREENWALD

EMOTIONAL MATURITY
in LOVE and MARRIAGE

Foreword by George S. Stevenson, M.D.

Harper & Brothers, New York

Library of Congress catalog card number: 61–8610

CONTENTS

FOREWORD

Many years ago I joined the staff of the gastrointestinal department in a medical school, suspecting that I would find there
many patients whose disorders were essentially emotional.
I was not disappointed.

The connection between the life problem and gastroen-
terology was sometimes physiological, as in cases of ulcer and
colitis, but often the patient applied to the gastrointestinal
department for help because he could not directly face and
talk about marital or sexual disorders and he hoped to receive
help without embarrassment, by a devious approach.

Problems of birth control, impotence, inability to feel
socially accepted (cases of acne and obesity) were hidden behind the complaint "fullness and gas." These people didn't go
to a gynecologist or a marriage counselor because this would
have forced them to face and talk about their problems directly.

Today, many such people may be helped to rise above
those reservations and shame by seeing that these intimate
aspects of life can be written about dispassionately and frankly,

as the authors of this book have done. This assurance will be a first step in the solution of their problem.

Other persons will still be unable to rise above the reserve with which they have lived for years, but will be encouraged to sit with an experienced professional person who can skillfully help them emerge from their fetters. Some will have much broader problems of mental health that are so general and basic that their feeling of shame is only a symptom of secondary importance. These are the mentally ill, or mentally ailing, who suffer in all aspects of living and who need general therapeutic help. Many mental health associations provide information and referral service for such people who are unable to unravel their quandaries. These associations can be appealed to for guidance.

There is difficulty on the part of some people in distinguishing between the serious popular presentation offered in this book, designed to help them, and the lurid or pornographic presentation. There will be some who, in spite of this book's serious presentation, will read for thrills just as they eavesdrop into medical books. But it is good to see this subject handled here in a forthright spirit that at no point savors of the lurid.

George S. Stevenson, M.D.

Vice-President (and incoming President) World Federation for Mental Health; past President, American Psychiatric Association; past Medical Director, National Association for Mental Health; past President, American Orthopsychiatric Association; Editor, *Mental Hygiene*

EMOTIONAL MATURITY
in LOVE and MARRIAGE

1 *THE CRISIS OF COURTSHIP*

Through the ages man has courted woman in many different ways, depending on the culture and the century. Even the duration of courtship has varied from place to place and over the years.

Courtship might be brief or it might sometimes last for years as it did among the American Plains Indians. There it even continued into marriage as the bride was further courted for weeks before the bridegroom attempted sexual intimacy, allowing her to know him in this new setting by merely lying quietly next to her each night. Newly married couples among the Thompson Indians of British Columbia, although sleeping under the same robe, were not supposed to consummate the marriage until from two to seven nights after the ceremony. In some tribes the bride slept for five nights in the company of her bridesmaids; in others, the mother of the bride sat in the bridal bedroom all night watching over the couple for a week, at the end of which time they were permitted to "know" each other, in the Biblical sense.

Today, in this country, the length of courtship varies. Some rush into marriage at once without troubling to examine their motives, and there are those who prolong the courtship many months, perhaps even years, while they explore their feelings. Most of us, however, measure out at least a few months before we march down the aisle.

Courtship is a time of testing, of finding out more about the loved one. If men and women took the trouble to become more deeply acquainted during courtship, they might be happier in marriage. Perhaps there would be fewer marriages, or perhaps the marriages would be to different people, but many experts believe the chance for success might be higher.

It is easy to become physically blind during courtship. A consuming passion for the loved one may drive all else out of mind. If we choose someone with whom we have little chance for happiness, we generally have sensed in advance the traits that will later cause the anguish. But either we pretend not to see them or we make excuses for them. We think, "He (or she) will change," or, more rarely, "This is something I will learn to bear."

During courtship some do not want to see the defects in the one they love whom they somehow must believe perfect, although a more mature love accepts a person as he is, faults and all. After a whirlwind courtship, one man married a woman he had known only four weeks, and within several months was telling a woman he had known for years, "I should have married you, but I was so desperately in love, it drove all reason out of my mind."

He voiced what was for him a profound truth. During courtship he became, like many who fall violently in love, deprived of sense, emotionally blind. He did not see clearly enough the woman he married. His use of the word "desperately" was significant. Why the desperation? Could it have been founded on the fear of facing the real world? "Desperate" is a word often used to describe feelings of love. If love is sudden and desperate, it is not likely to be based on what is lasting and real.

The urgency that so often accompanies falling in love may override common sense. Some psychoanalysts call the state of love pathological because it is so far removed from normal. People often behave differently from the way they usually do. They may "walk on clouds." They may lose the desire to eat. They may become impervious to frustrations that would ordinarily bother them. They may react more intensely to all emotions, tears as well as laughter.

Sex Before Marriage

Courtship poses many problems for both men and women, the chief one of which, in this day of greater sexual freedom, probably is the question of whether there should be sexual intimacy before marriage. What was the practice of primitive man? A look at the customs of our ancestors somehow gives us a clearer understanding of ourselves as we see man minus the masks of civilization.

Primitive tribes varied in their attitude toward chastity before marriage. Among some primitive peoples the young woman was scrupulously kept from any sexual contact until she was married and any breach of chastity was punished by death. But in other tribes both sexes were permitted to enjoy sexual freedom prior to marriage. Some even considered sexual intimacy a preliminary to marriage, a trial before the establishment of a permanent relationship, perhaps to find out literally whether the marriage would be fruitful. The man either took the woman to his home or went to live with her and her parents for a certain length of time before marrying.

This is similar to the proposal made in this country several years ago when Judge Ben Lindsey advocated companionate or trial marriage. He suggested that people try each other out for a year or so before "renewing the option" and getting permanently married. Some use easy divorce as a way of making a trial marriage.

A generation ago in this country little conflict would have existed over the question of sexual intimacy before marriage. Most women did not permit any intimacy beyond the chaste kiss until the marriage vows were spoken. But, as Kinsey has shown us, it is not uncommon for couples to be sexually intimate with others before deciding on a mate, a trend that seems to be increasing. Does this harm the chance for a successful marriage?

The premature consummation of sex, that is, before a real relationship has been established, often prevents a man and a woman from becoming acquainted with each other. An intense sexual affair not only keeps deeper feelings from developing but blinds one to the many other pleasures that may be present.

When a man and woman make love the first night they meet, that may well end any chance at permanence. Many authorities believe that an important part of love is the inhibition of sexual expression and that the unfulfilled sexual feelings add a strength and a dimension to love. Love, they say, needs to be built on many psychic fronts before the final intimacy occurs. It is like the frosting on a cake, added last, after the substance has been formed.

Many of our conventions arise out of centuries of experience as to what is believed best for both man and society. The custom that couples restrain themselves from engaging in sexual intimacy before marriage is thus believed to be a wise one psychologically. One very practical reason for its existence, as far as the woman is concerned, is that the acute sexual desire in the man which remains unsatisfied adds fire to his wish to marry her and he reaches a point where he is willing to give up everything just to possess her. Perhaps this is sad, although true, that a woman's refusal to indulge in sex accounts for many marriages, for by itself it is surely not a solid reason for marrying and will not hold together a marriage that lacks the other essentials.

The woman who breaks society's rules may experience a sense of guilt no matter how she may excuse what she does. This guilt will destroy much of her delight, both in the man and in the sexual intimacy. And, no matter how liberal intellectually the man or woman, there will often exist the erosive feeling that, should the woman permit intimacy before marriage, she is wanton. She may be thought of as "a bad woman" both by her lover and herself because she could not control herself until they were legally bound to each other.

This is not always true, for there are some who know themselves well enough to be sure of the permanence of their feelings for the other person. They sense the richness of the one who is beloved and are not blinded by physical desire. However, these are rare souls in our society.

Marriage Is No Tea Party

But sexual intimacy before marriage is not the criterion of whether the marriage will be successful, although it is important. The criterion is how well we know ourselves and, therefore, how well we are able to know each other, at least to sense each other's capacity for love, tenderness, and understanding so that we are willing to make the compromises necessary for life together.

Many authorities believe that the more we know ourselves,

the better our chance of making a wise choice of a mate and the less struggle there will probably be in achieving a happy marriage. We will feel less exploited and less exploiting. We will have selected on the basis of real needs, not our fantasies and unrealizable ideals.

Getting to know someone fully takes a long, long time. It is a lifetime venture. To grow closer to someone year after year, in affection, companionship, and respect—this is love. Love that lasts does not spring full-blown at first sight. Even the best of marriages requires that each partner work at it some of the time.

When an unwise choice is made, one does not particularly want to know the other fully, for he will not like what he finds. After a few months of marriage, if one discovers the other is selfish, thoughtless, and insensitive, there seems little joy or value in getting to know him any better.

There are some who seem to grasp the total personality of the other in one small glimpse. These people seem to have the capacity to sense the broad outlines of the other's character and use the later acquaintanceship to fill in the details. Perhaps many more of us would possess this skill, often called intuition, if we permitted ourselves to acknowledge our own feelings and emotions.

One highly intuitive man described the process as follows: "When I meet someone, I feel something. I look at this feeling and figure out what the other person is doing to arouse this feeling. By studying my reactions I learn about the other person. My reactions are based on cues I pick up from the other person, such as the quality of his voice, the way he holds his body, or how he eats. Any of these items which I observe without awareness of my observation may serve to trigger off feelings which I then study to understand the other person." Described in this manner, intuition is a natural rather than a mystical process, based in large part on the insight gained from past experiences.

Marriage cannot always be a tea party. It makes many demands on each partner and it is not easy to adapt to the adjustments usually required for a happy marriage. If we feel too threatened in that the mate demands more than we are capable of giving, we will seek escape and greater comfort elsewhere.

According both to divorce statistics and the number of married people who live apart, many are not able to make the compromises necessary to live with their mates in comparative comfort and peace. They are not emotionally ready for marriage and the marriage is doomed from the start, even before the start—in courtship.

Courtship cannot be a time of certainty, but it can be a time to recognize clues as to the flexibility of oneself and the other, clues that will indicate whether the marriage will result either in happiness or failure.

While engaging in sexual intimacy is apt to cloud the clues, there is always the exception that proves the rule. One woman refused to allow her fiancé to make love to her before they were married, insisting it would ruin their chance for happiness. They were married following six months of courtship. Then she discovered her husband was impotent. She must have sensed this before the marriage but was afraid to discover it in actuality lest the marriage be called off. She would have spared herself much grief had she attempted sexual intimacy, found out the truth, and broken the engagement or encouraged him to seek help, for impotence is rarely an insoluble problem with skilled professional aid.

Sometimes a courtship ends abruptly as one or the other realizes the marriage would not be successful. One man pursued a woman with whom he thought he was in love, asking her whether she would marry him if he divorced his wife to whom he had been married twenty years. She consented and he instituted proceedings. While the outcome was still pending, he and his intended bride went away together for a week to attend a business conference, during which time he introduced her to many of his associates who had known his wife. He felt their disapproval for, while they could understand his having a mistress, they did not forgive him for bringing her to a conference where their wives were present. He did not tell them he intended to marry her, for he thought the damage had been done and nothing would rectify it. He knew he felt very uncomfortable about the whole affair and when his fiancée told him she had changed her mind about marrying him, he was not surprised, although he tried to convince her otherwise.

When they returned home and she still refused to marry him, he realized he felt relieved and wondered if he had taken her on this trip knowing in advance its outcome, or perhaps hoping this would be the outcome. He admitted to himself that he really did not want to marry her for a number of reasons which he then was able to face, including a tendency on her part to dominate him. The illicit trip had brought to the surface many underlying conflicts between them.

The Rush-Hour Marriage

Most people marry because they believe themselves in love. They careen through courtship, hurtle through the honeymoon, and plunge into the prosaic business of living together. Then, all too often, deep disillusionment destroys the romantic spell and they are left tragically wondering what torpedoed their passionate love.

It might have been wiser if they had been able to do a

little wondering beforehand, to examine the reasons why they were marrying. Were they rushing into an unrewarding intimacy without knowing what they were doing? Or were they thoughtfully undertaking a lifetime relationship, prepared to accept a certain amount of frustration and disillusionment, not asking that the marriage be perfect, not asking that their partner give them a love they had never received elsewhere?

If people feel they have never received love, and their hunger for it is great, they will find it difficult to be satisfied by the love they are able to obtain in marriage. For if marriage is undertaken out of a hungry need for love, it faces difficulties. Many who speak of their great need for love may be looking for rejection, for instance. They ask for so much that they often exhaust even the capacity of the most giving, in order to triumphantly demonstrate that no one "really cares."

"I need you," one man told a woman. "That's why I'm marrying you."

At that moment she felt elated that she was the one woman in the world who could fulfill his need, but months after the marriage she realized that his need was not a sufficient foundation for the marriage because it was a selfish, demanding thing which, she felt, did not allow room for her rights.

To want to be needed may be an equally unhappy motive for marriage. Often what it really means is, "I need to be needed." The unwed woman or man who says sadly, "No one needs me," or the mother who feels her children no longer need her and sinks into a depression, may really be saying they need someone to fill the emptiness in their life. One first needs to be needed by the self. One must first fulfill one's own needs, before being capable of fulfilling anybody else's. The person who is complete within himself, not screaming to the world of his loneliness, never has to live alone. The one who is always bemoaning his great need for someone to love is ever alone.

Some, in their war against loneliness, indulge in an endless, blind search for affection, as though starved for physical contact and willing to take it wherever they find it, from anyone who shows the slightest response. They must have somebody (some body) to touch and to feel, as if to reassure themselves they are alive. This is a kind of "contact hunger," the intense desire for physical intimacy as often displayed by the promiscuous man or woman.

The feeling exists to some degree in all of us, for we could not live without contact with others. If a child grows up alone in a forest, having no physical or psychological contact with another human being, he will probably turn out feeble-minded, if indeed he survives at all. A man condemned to complete isolation will start to hallucinate before long and, if left there indefinitely, may go mad.

One of the difficulties encountered in the training of astronauts has been to help them endure long stretches of solitude. Today's experiments are invalid to a certain extent because, while they cause the men temporary inconvenience, every astronaut in training knows that the minute he feels he cannot bear the isolation any longer and cries "Help!" he will be released from the cell.

The cry that some mistake as love is really the cry of "Help!" as they strain to break away from a psychic isolation that makes them feel imprisoned within an emotional cave. They crave a companion with whom to share life. When this is the core of love, we may wonder whether such people are able to create a lasting marriage. Theirs is not a wise choice of a compatible mate but a demand that someone rescue them from a loneliness they can no longer bear.

Such are the men and women who shriek, "All I want is somebody to love me!" *All I want is somebody to love me—* as though this were a modest demand when it is asking the impossible. The only way to get rewarding love seems to be to give it. The moment it is demanded, it is apt to weaken.

It is probably not wise to marry only because you want someone to love you, as it is not wise to believe marriage will solve all your problems, or help you escape loneliness. It is also probably not wise to marry because you wish the status of marriage, or desire someone with whom to share life, or want someone to take care of you, or feel pity and sympathy for the other and want to take care of him. It may not be wise to hope marriage will enable you to feel less guilty about sex, or believe it will stop you from being promiscuous, or permit you to have sexual intimacy heretofore impossible because of your inhibitions. Your signature on a marriage license does not usually change you significantly.

If any one, or several, of the above are the only reasons for wanting to get married, there need be no surprise if the marriage turns out unhappily. These all mask hidden, deeper motives that are dangerous to marriage. The deeper reasons do not show themselves until after marriage when they often explode like bombshells to blast the idyllic bliss of courtship days.

"You were so sweet to me *before* we were married," a wife bitterly accuses her husband.

"You were so different then," he retorts.

Both are right—half-right. They *were* different, in that they allowed only part of their natures to show. During courtship they attempted to conceal the part they did not like, and believed no one else would like either. But in the closeness of day-to-day living, the concealed part often appears and causes emotional havoc, if it does not actually wreck the marriage. They could put on an act with each other only so long.

Since we are all human, we are more alike than we are different. The problem usually is not that we have repellent areas of our personality but that in a mistaken notion that we must be perfect, we hide our normal human weaknesses, and just as sometimes the cure is worse than the illness, so the mask may be more terrifying than the weakness it hides.

Love Does Not Have To Be Blind

In a good relationship there should be little need to act, to play games with the other. Each one should be able to be himself, confident the other will accept him as he is.

The one who is emotionally mature does not have to bother constantly to play a part—for himself or for others. He knows and accepts his imperfections and he also trusts his mate to accept him in spite of them.

Why is one person emotionally mature, another not? It is a cliché by now to say that you are emotionally mature if you like and accept your own self and therefore are able to like and accept others, but clichés often hold the grain of truth. If you like and accept yourself, you have nothing to conceal from yourself or others and thus nothing to fear. You know you are human, which means you possess strange, savage desires as do all men, but you are able to control them and use your energy wisely.

What keeps someone from liking himself? There are many reasons for self-hatred, most of them stemming from conflicts of childhood days. If one has not felt beloved by parents as one grows up, he does not feel worthy of love. And if he marries for a reason he knows unworthy, this adds to his self-hatred. He cannot help but know in his heart that he has not married out of love, but for selfish reasons. Only as he is able to admit this and face his true motives for marriage may he deal with his feelings honestly and become more able to be tender and affectionate.

Would that it were as easy to write about emotional maturity as about sexual technique! Books by the dozen on sexual behavior contain countless suggestions on how to make love. They give specific instructions as "Take Leg A and put over Leg B and—"

But advice on emotional maturity, without which, incidentally, sexual maturity is rarely possible, is not so easily given. One cannot outline steps A, B, and C to emotional maturity because it deals with a feeling that is elusive and undescribable, half of mind, half of body, a feeling that poets and philosophers and novelists have tried to put into words through the ages. Love.

Man has ever been confused about the stuff of love. If all the books describing and discussing it were laid end to end, they would reach to the top of Mount Everest. Love seems to mean all things to all men—even murder has been justified in the name of love.

Wars are fought, countries conquered, people killed daily by one another, supposedly for love. "I couldn't live without him, so I shot him when he said he was going to leave me." "She betrayed me with another man and I strangled her." "We are going to occupy this nation because it needs our protection and affection so its people may become free."

But is it love when men must die because of it? When Wilde wrote, "For each man kills the thing he loves," was he speaking only of love? Was it not, rather, the mixture of love and hate which many experience at one time or another toward those who are close?

Psychoanalysts, whose goal is to help men become better able to love, have clarified the concepts of love and hate. We know now that both are powerful drives and that often hate and love are inextricably intertwined.

We are born able to express anger so that we may survive. Our screams of rage as a baby tell our mother when something hurts us or we are starving for food. It is the only way a baby possesses of communicating with his mother when something goes wrong.

But the expression of love we must learn. We learn it over the years, gradually finding out that to live harmoniously with someone else we must give up some of the love of self which enabled us to endure the harsh years of childhood, and harsh they are, for it is not easy to become civilized.

There are two kinds of love. There is the popular image of love as visualized in the movies and much of our fiction, which is a hungry, demanding, desperate love, more like the love of a child for its mother, a love propelled by its own needs. Quite different from it in quality is the mature or adult love, which is understanding, compassionate, friendly and, above all, tender.

Mature love fuses tender feelings with feelings of physical desire. Some mistake lust alone for love. Sensuality by itself is not enough for love. It must be combined with tenderness. If we are able to unite tenderness and sensuality, we are able to love maturely. If we cannot achieve the fusion but must split the two feelings, we are doomed to unhappiness in trying to love or be loved, or we may suffer from sexual frigidity or promiscuity.

Love does not have to be blind. When it is blind, it is not love. For when it is blind, it is often not love of another but only narrow love of self. One usually sees the beloved clearly if one sees the self clearly.

The Threats of Love

One conflict that may become apparent during courtship comes from being torn between the wish to fill the emptiness of life by sharing it with someone else and the fear that this may mean a sacrifice of one's identity.

Many who are lonely insist they do not like living in solitude and would give it up in a second if they could only find someone to love. But the fact remains they have chosen this way of life and their choice is made, in part, to protect themselves against what they feel might be invasion by another person. It is difficult to live with someone, no matter how sensitive, how thoughtful, how lovable he may be. Some psychic distress will have to be endured at one time or another.

Pressures fall on all of us to get married, to accept the inescapable pain and try to cope with it. There is both the impersonal pressure of society and the personal pressure of parents, and the one who is unable to marry often cannot help but feel the pariah of the century.

Some parents are not even subtle about their wishes. There are mothers who complain sorrowfully to daughters who sit around the house on Saturday night, "You don't have a date?" as though the daughter were a fatal failure who would send her mother to an early grave if she were not soon courted by some eligible man. Sometimes the mother's demand that the daughter marry may prevent the marriage in that the daughter, angered, decides to avenge herself against her mother by *not* marrying.

Most mothers do not worry so much about sons; therefore the bachelor lives under less of a social stigma than the spinster. One young woman of twenty-three sought out a graduate school to earn her Ph.D. so she could be called "Dr." because she cringed every time someone hailed her as "Miss."

But there are those who ignore social and personal pressures and refuse to marry because they are too afraid of involvements they believe will be painful. They prefer to cope with loneliness rather than risk the pain that accompanies closeness. They see the loneliness as the lesser of the two evils.

Why must there be some pain in a close relationship? For two reasons, each extremely significant in our emotional life.

First, there is the fear of loss of identity, of being engulfed and swallowed. "If I get married I won't be free to live as I wish" (both men and women). "I won't be allowed out with the boys whenever I feel like it" (men). "I won't be free to work, I'll be chained to the kitchen" (women).

The young man or woman about to get married has spent his or her whole life up to this point in trying to establish a sense of identity. This entails breaking away from the family, a process that involves pain, which most of us seek to escape. We are pleasure-bent, not pain-bent.

But pain, like every other feeling, is part of survival. Pain has its purpose in helping to keep us alive. If we did not find it painful when we accidentally thrust our hand into a fire, we would not remove it and our hand would be eaten up by flames. If we did not fear pain, we would calmly let a truck or car strike us, crippling or perhaps killing us. One difference between inanimate and animate matter is that living matter is capable of sensation, both pleasure and pain.

As he strives to become an individual in his own right, the child causes his parents pain when he retorts, "I won't!" Until the time he is able to say this, he is only an extension of his parents, doing what they wish. But when he finally takes the step and says, "I won't," to his parents' command that he eat the cornflakes or the spinach, he is trying to establish his identity. He is expressing a wish of his own and if he is not then verbally slaughtered by shrieks and screams, or physically slapped, he develops naturally. Wise parents may insist he eat the cornflakes or spinach but they do this quietly, either by distracting his attention and feeding him or, preferably, waiting until he is hungry enough to eat anything.

If parents do not express undue anger at a child's attempts to set out on his own, he will not become angry in retaliation. Every child is angry enough to wish to kill when frustrated, and this anger he must learn to bear because frustration is inevitable. But there is another anger, one inspired by selfish, psychically or physically brutal parents, which is far harder for a child to understand and handle. He is apt to repress it and then it explodes at others later in life.

The subtle "I won'ts" of growing up—"I won't wear the red dress, I want to wear the blue one" or "I won't come home at eight when all the other kids are allowed out until nine"— are the wishes a child expresses so he can feel that he, too, is an individual. If the carrying out of these wishes harms him or others, it is his parents' right and duty to step in and control him, but in a gentle, understanding way. The manner in which they administer discipline makes all the difference in the world. It is the difference in later years between an angry, frightened human being and a thoughtful, tender one.

For some, this developing individuality, not yet complete, is threatened by falling in love, for to be close to someone implies that we will have to yield to his wishes sometimes and please him so he will continue to love us. As a child we may have been told by our parents that if we did not bow to their wishes we would lose their love; therefore, when we grow up, becoming involved with another person is accompanied by the age-old fear that we must give up many of our wishes to keep peace.

This is why some retreat in order not to love. The concept

of "togetherness" made many wince because it frightened them. They did not want to be *that* together. They wanted to be able to keep their identity even within marriage and family.

The second cause of pain, a pull in the opposite direction, is called "separation anxiety." It is first experienced at birth when the baby must adjust to being pulled out of the comfortable womb where all its needs have been met without any effort on its part. It wants to be set free yet it fears separation from the maternal warmth. This occurs again at the time of weaning. The child may want to start eating by itself, to be on its own, and yet fear the loss of the mother's bodily comfort which the weaning brings.

All future relationships that are close carry this dread of separation. If someone is not dear to you, you can easily forsake him or be forsaken by him without any anxiety, but if someone is important and abandons you, it is as though your world fell apart.

One man loved dogs and for years kept one in his home. But every so often when a dog died, he went through agony at the loss. Finally he decided to do without a dog and thus avoid the pain of separation. This was a man who had lost his mother in early childhood so that each time a dog died, he once again lived through his mother's death and the misery of the final separation from her.

In any human relationship lurks the threat of separation, for the loved one may die or you may die, he may leave you or you may leave him, for whatever reason. Some feel it is too dangerous to become involved with anyone and will make no alliances, denying themselves the myriad pleasures of living with someone for fear of the pain that would follow a possible loss.

Anxiety over separation occurs in many forms, some minor

but nonetheless painful. One man who had been on a strict diet, under doctor's orders to lose weight, came home from work eager to tell his wife, who usually was there to greet him, about a successful business deal. He found she had unexpectedly gone to visit a sick aunt and left the note: "Darling, salvage from the icebox whatever you should eat for dinner. I'll be home about ten."

Distraught, feeling abandoned, he hurled his diet overboard and started to eat his way through the icebox. When he was a small boy and his mother left the house, as she often did to shop or visit friends, he had felt this same despair. Then, the maid in whose care he had been left, would keep him quiet by stuffing him with candy and ice cream. When this fear of being deserted by someone he needed occurred later in life, even though he knew it was unreal, he again took to food as solace, though it was bad for his health. Some people act just the opposite, refusing to eat at all as they become depressed over what they feel a desertion. The choice of reaction seems to depend upon which one they found useful as a child.

Some fight abandonment by acting with abandon, plunging into promiscuity or drinking or gambling. They feel inside that as long as no one cares what happens to them, they cannot care about themselves and, in a sense, throw their lives away.

Another way to deal with anxiety over separation is to become the instigator of the separation instead of the victim. Rather than risk the other person's leaving you, you make sure to leave him first. A well-known way of mastering anxiety is to undertake the threatening deed yourself, beating the other to the fearful punch. This is shown by those who have one affair after another, jilting the partner before they are dumped.

Some who are fundamentally fearful of life may act on the

fear by undertaking dangerous deeds. Those who become stunt men and daredevils are often inwardly terrified of danger and death and try to handle their fear by facing the terror and overcoming it, as though to deny it exists. Similarly, those deeply afraid of separation may attempt to allay their fear by separating frequently, using the familiar "protesting too much" technique.

Because of these two fears—loss of identity and the pain of separation—during courtship some feel they must not allow the other to become too sure of them. The result may be a complicated emotional dance.

A man meets a woman at a cocktail party, thinks she is attractive, takes down her telephone number and a few days later calls up and asks, "How about dinner?" Afterward he takes her for a drive in his car and as they roll along the highway and talk, he discovers he likes her very much, wants to know her better and tells her so.

But she does not trust him, or herself, as yet and shows only mild interest. She is popular, has a number of suitors, and conveys this information to him subtly. However he is persistent and keeps calling, so she decides he is a candidate for her heart because his intentions seem serious. She is pleased when she takes him to a party and notices that the other women cast approving looks at him.

Then what happens? He does not call for a week. She becomes alarmed over what she did wrong. Was she too anxious? Did she show her affection too much or not enough? Perhaps she let him kiss her too ardently that first night and now he has lost respect for her.

After days that draw out like years, he calls but merely to ask how she is. She tells him she has missed him, but now he seems totally disinterested. She decides it is hopeless and she has made a mistake in believing he cared. She goes out with another man, managing to let him know that she is back in circulation through a mutual friend. As soon as he finds this out, he calls immediately and asks for a date. She decides not to appear eager, then when her interest is again revived he becomes distant, and so it goes, back and forth, like a dance movement.

What are the reasons for this trying, painful play-acting characteristic of a number of courtships to some degree? It is the fear of becoming too involved and having to give up one's identity, and also fear of the anxiety over losing someone beloved. As soon as the fear eases, which occurs when the person seems unattainable, the original attraction returns.

In courtship the man is usually the aggressor as he tries to gain the favor of the woman by wooing her. The woman, however, does not remain completely passive. She may have in the first place invited his approach and may reward his aggression with certain demure concessions. There are those men who claim that the woman proposed to them, perhaps jokingly, perhaps seriously, but these are men who do not wish to take the responsibility of marriage and must place the blame on the woman for the desire to get married. Despite the conventional attitude marriage is more a woman's business than a man's, the subject of marriage often first broached by the woman.

Some Cannot Love

Another problem that may exist in courtship is that of an incipient competition which becomes full-blown in marriage. The woman thinks, "He sat in my apartment and watched television all last Saturday night so tonight he can take me dancing." Or the man muses, "I bought expensive tickets to a Broadway show last week so tonight she can at least cook me a steak dinner." This bookkeeping is part of the competitive spirit, a bargaining that may take place in the name of love but which hardly conveys the idea of love as a gift.

A popular notion of the way in which the battle of the sexes expresses itself is that in courtship women hold out against sexual intimacy while men are eternally trying to seduce them. It is confusing to some women to discover there are men who do not want to make love to them before marriage, and to some men to discover there are woman willing to indulge in sexual intimacy with or without demanding marriage as payment.

To some men and women courtship, instead of ending in marriage, becomes an everlasting stage. Rather than a way station on the path to marriage, it turns into a haven in which they seek to dwell forever. Such are the Don Juans and their feminine counterparts who fly from one affair to another, ephemeral as the butterfly flitting from flower to flower. They are dedicated to courtship and spend their lives in pursuit of it, afraid of the intimacy and responsibility which a deep love would bring.

They are never truly happy with anyone. To them the conquest is the thing. They do not want to know themselves or whoever it is to whom they are momentarily making love. Such people often wind up at the age of fifty or fifty-five wailing over agonizing loneliness in a world of their own chaotic making.

One man, now approaching forty-five, has engaged in a series of love affairs, not just one at a time but two. He is perpetually involved with two women, both of whom are "lovely girls, not at all like the other horrible women I've known." He can never decide which of the two he will marry and is always asking his friends to choose for him. He succeeds in dividing everyone he knows into two armed camps, each cheering for their candidate of the moment, while he goes merrily on his way not even trying to make up his mind. Obviously he has little wish to get married.

Another perennial bachelor complains, "I just can't find a woman who is real, who will be kind and decent. All the women I meet are monsters." He is always involved with a woman but she is never "the right one."

Just as common is the complaint often uttered by unmarried women who ask, "Where do you find a real man? They're all married. The ones I know are either impotent or homosexual or promiscuous, what I call 'ineligible bachelors.' " These women often engage in one affair after another in their search for "a real man" or will have nothing to do with any man, "real" or no.

The "real" woman usually has less trouble finding a "real" man and vice versa. Those dissatisfied with every member of the opposite sex are in their hearts really dissatisfied with themselves. The perfect partner would not suit them, if such were to exist.

Not even to try to love is dooming the self to the hell of loneliness. The purpose of love is to be able to love, and those who cannot do this live as though in desolation on a desert isle.

To refuse to love is almost as if one refused life, turning one's back on it. The greatest of all needs is to be loved and to give love, to be deeply involved with a member of the opposite sex, to feel that we share in another's dreams and achievements and the other shares equally in ours.

There is probably no more devastating pain than that of being perpetually alone, yet thousands choose this tortured existence in preference to marriage. There is the bachelor who jumps from woman to woman, and the bachelor who will have nothing to do with any woman, and the bachelor who seeks only men. There are women who show the same tendencies, either turning to promiscuity, or refusing to tolerate any man, or finding warmth only in the arms of another woman.

These are all people afraid of mature love. They have grown up unable to learn how to give love or receive it. They are caught in the fantasies of their early years and only psychological help* will enable them to fight free of their illusions.

But each year hundreds of thousands of men and women manage to overcome whatever fears they possess and get married. They pass safely through courtship, the narrow channel into the sea of matrimony. They know they will emerge into waters which, though often calm and serene, will sometimes be quite stormy.

They look on marriage, however, as a fascinating journey and the stormy seas as a challenge to be met, rather than a disaster from which to withdraw and sit in solitude and sadness on the lonely shore.

---

* The term "psychological help" as used throughout this book refers to help with emotional problems that may be given by psychoanalysts, psychologists, or psychiatrists. It may be either "deep therapy," which may last from three to five years five times a week, or psychotherapy, sometimes lasting only a few months, once a week, or six or eight people discussing their problems with a professional.

2 THE MYTH OF THE
HAPPY HONEYMOON

A crucial test of adjustment comes during the honeymoon, for it is then each feels the first impact of the other's needs and demands. A distance bound to lend enchantment lies between them up until the moment the newlyweds face each other in the hotel room. But the distance narrows as they achieve the closeness they desire.

This is a closeness from which eventually they may wish to escape at times. For it is one thing for a man and a woman to be deeply in love when they do not collide in the conflicts of day-to-day living, but it is quite another to remain in love in spite of the irritations and frustrations that are destined to arise when two people live together, even if both possess the patience of Job.

Traditionally, honeymoons are visualized as harboring only moments of poignant pleasure that mount into hours of delirious delight. They are designed to transport bride and bridegroom far from the sordid world of reality to the solitude of mountaintop or seashore cove where they may learn to know each other in the splendor of seclusion. Sometimes the knowing comes easily, sometimes not, and then the honeymoon turns into a time of trial and torture.

If too much is expected or feared, the honeymoon may become a horror. Sometimes such a build-up occurs that the emotional letdown afterward is apt to be devastating. Many men and women go through the excitement of elaborate preparation for the wedding, and then there is the drama of the wedding day itself. We, as indeed did our ancestors, primitive men, make of weddings a public spectacle, each wedding attempting to outshine every other wedding in history in food, drink, and fashion.

Actually the lavishness of weddings serves a purpose. It gives wide publicity to the union of the man and the woman, distinguishing their relationship as a recognized marriage as contrasted with an illicit love affair. Legality is a process of which to be proud, and bride and bridegroom want to tell the world of their uniting. In some primitive tribes in Africa, the bridegroom consummates the marriage in full view of a number of girls and women, whereas affairs are conducted in secret.

To protect the state of marriage in every society, a man and woman who behave as if they were married without the proper social sanction are made to feel outcasts. There are always some rebels who insist on taking the opposite viewpoint, making a virtue of not conforming. Thus one woman, when asked by a new acquaintance at a party, "Are you and Joe married?" drew herself up indignantly, as though her honor were being insulted, and replied, "Please, I'm an anarchist." But she is the exception to the rule.

Incidentally, the throwing of rice at a newly married couple traces back to the primitive custom of hurling some kind of cereal, grain, or dried fruit on the bride. This prevailed from India and Indo-China westward to the Atlantic Ocean. One modern adaptation is confetti.

The custom arose, some authorities believe, out of a wish to promote fecundity, the seed-bearing grasses and fruits symbolizing the seeds of the masculine body. Therefore, when we throw rice at bride and bridegroom, we are saying, "We hope you have a lot of children." In Bohemia and Silesia today, it is believed that the number of grains of peeled barley afterward found lying on the bride's gown, indicates the number of children to whom she will give birth.

Some find it difficult to shift quickly from their starring role in the supposedly once-in-a-lifetime performance before a minister and capacity crowd, to the realistic role they must accept with only each other as audience after they become man and wife. It would be hard for a honeymoon not to turn into somewhat of an anticlimax after the hoopla of most weddings.

Honeymoon Jitters

The honeymoon may hold critical hours if both bride and bridegroom embark on it with fear and anxiety. Then they will find it difficult to relax and enjoy each other. Frequently if one member of a couple is unhappy, the other also will be, although he may hide it more successfully.

We may question the concept of the honeymoon as grotesque and unreal, but honeymoons have been with us for a long time so they must serve some purpose. The word originated, according to Webster in cynical mood, in reference to the mutual affection of newlyweds which waned like the moon. The German word for honeymoon, *Flitterwochen,* means tinsel weeks, another apt description.

The honeymoon has come to connote uninhibited and constant sexual pleasure according to the jokes about it which usually focus on the poor, wan, exhausted bridegroom who flies up with the window shade. The very name "Niagara Falls," this country's honeymoon mecca, brings a snicker when it is mentioned. Many honeymooners do not want the world to know their status. They feel ashamed, as though everyone who discovers they are on a honeymoon will picture them making love day and night.

When one bridegroom proudly informed the clerk of a hotel, "We're honeymooners," his bride blushed and whispered to him in embarrassment, "Did you *have* to tell him?"

The honeymoon holds two main challenges. It is a time of facing sudden closeness with someone who is almost a stranger. It also represents a break from all that has been familiar in one's life. "Forsaking all others" is the vow of both bride and bridegroom, and this means giving up one's first allegiance to mother and father and sisters and brothers and uncles and aunts and grandparents and every relative alive.

There is bound to be a certain sadness at leaving as if forever, emotionally, those who have been nearest and dearest. This also brings the realization that one is no longer a child but an adult. No longer has one a right to *be* mothered. One must prepare to *be* a mother, or a father.

If, at this time, the fear of separation from parents is too deep, the loneliness will be difficult to combat. Some brides yearn so greatly for their mothers and fathers that they will telephone them daily, or write them long letters, or perhaps even cut the honeymoon short so they may be reunited sooner. Or, perhaps, it is the husband who calls his mother "just to say hello," or to inform her "we're all right," really telling her how much he misses her.

There may be a tendency to fight this loneliness by demanding too much from the other to fill the void. Some brides resent the fact that their husbands, instead of reveling in this new-found happiness with a soul mate, want to leave them for a few hours to play golf or swim. One bride said bitterly, "My husband, instead of spending his time with me, preferred to read some ten-year-old magazines he found in the junk pile behind the cabin. It seemed he wanted to do anything but pay attention to me." This may be reversed and the husband may become jealous of the attention his wife gives elsewhere, wanting to be the only one she notices.

The demand for full-time concern from the other is not a wise one for it allows the other no freedom to make his or her own choice. No one can or should turn over all his energy and time to someone else. This is slavery, not love.

Familiarity may breed either contempt or greater love, depending on those involved. By the time the honeymoon has ended, perhaps each feels slightly disappointed in the other. The bride may think that instead of the Prince Charming she thought she had married—the willing slave who would anticipate her every wish and rush to fulfill it—her husband is more like Mephistopheles. The bridegroom may be amazed to discover that the princess of his dreams, so sweet and appealing during courtship, is more like a witch who is bent on dominating him.

With some, from the first day of the honeymoon onwards, it is as though they were engaged in a subtle, never-ending battle for power and control. It begins with small struggles such as, "Why don't you put the suitcase here where it will be out of the way?" or "Aren't two drinks enough for you before supper?"

The Clash of Compulsions

The honeymoon asks a lot of both bride and bridegroom. Each must try to maintain his own identity yet please the other and, in so doing, give up some of his cherished, selfish idiosyncrasies.

One man who had lived alone for years was accustomed to flinging off his clothes and leaving them where they landed. As he did thus on his honeymoon, he saw a look of alarm and displeasure on his bride's face at his display of sloppiness. He stooped to pick up the discarded clothes and placed them neatly in closet and bureau, thinking this was but a slight concession to make for someone he loved.

In turn, his wife, who usually spent half an hour putting on make-up, when she realized how impatient her husband became after ten minutes, gave up the luxury of time and speeded up the process just so he would not be irritated.

These were but little deeds yet they marked the first attempts at compromise, at knowing what disturbed the other person and trying to make life more comfortable for him.

There is another way to handle the same situation which may be successful if the couple feel secure enough with each other. The untidy husband, noticing his wife's disturbed look, might have said to her, "Darling, I know this bothers you, but this is the way I am. I am not going to change nor do I expect you to change if something you do irritates me. You can either pick up my clothes for me—just as I will wait for you even though you spend hours putting on make-up—or you can become accustomed to having things strewn around the room and accept it as part of me."

The wise wife, the wife who accepts herself, is able to follow either of these suggestions, perhaps varying them, sometimes picking up after her husband, sometimes uncompulsively allowing his clothes to remain where they fall. In time, he may even decide to put his clothes away neatly, his own conviction that this is easier for him and keeps the clothes in better shape.

The first clash of compulsions (everyone has a few) occurs on the honeymoon. Either the bride and bridegroom are able more or less to accept each other's deeply rooted habits, which means fully accepting each other, or they are unable and unwilling, and if the latter, the rift may slowly widen, perhaps eventually ending months or years later in divorce or separation.

On the honeymoon, jealousy may first rear its hideous head. The husband may stare too longingly at a shapely red-head or the wife gaze too admiringly at the many-muscled lifeguard. Jealousy is a feeling we all possess and it must be controlled if we are to live in peace with someone. There will be moments when other members of the opposite sex appear attractive to one's mate, but if we feel secure with the one we love we will either not be jealous of his or her occasional glance elsewhere, or more probably accept our jealousy as the normal emotion it is, recognizing that it is only human to admire beauty of form, male and female. We cannot ask those we love to go through life wearing blinders and seeing only us, nor can we expect never to feel amazed that we are not enough, but we can try not to get involved in bitter quarrels about it.

Sex Rears Its Fearful Head

The honeymoon is a different thing to different people. Some feel overwhelmed by a beauty and fulfillment they never expected, hoping it will last. Others find the honeymoon disappointing. Still others accept it as what they had expected.

The fear of expressing one's sexual feelings, if present, usually first appears on the honeymoon. There are two main forms this fear may take—either a refusal to engage in sexual intimacy or a compulsion to overindulge.

One woman made such exorbitant sexual demands of her bridegroom that he complained, "I thought I married a fragile bird. 'Bird' is right—vulture. She was constantly after me to go up to our room. She just would not leave me alone."

When sexual desire becomes this intense, fear may be driving it. This bride suffered from the fear that she was unsuccessful as a sexual partner and that it was necessary for her to excel in the amorous act to prove she was feminine. She was putting the stress on quantity, not quality. When sex is used to "prove" something, it often lacks the tender, loving feeling that makes it fully enjoyable.

The fear of engaging in any sexual intimacy at all, or great reluctance, may be due to the newness of the situation or inherent shyness and wears off as one comes to know the mate and the pleasure increases. But if it persists beyond the honeymoon for any length of time, psychiatric help might be sought, for such fear is frequently indicative of deep sexual conflicts which the person would have difficulty in solving alone.

Some who feel threatened by their sexual feelings will respond to them with fear and anger. They will find no serenity in closeness but rather imbue it with the aura of warfare. They feel they must prove themselves, or that they are being exploited, or resent that they must give up a part of themselves, rather than wanting to give of themselves out of affection.

They will not want to compromise, which they must learn to do in order to live with someone. To compromise is not the same as being forced to "give in." There is all the difference in the world between "compromising," a thoughtful, conscious gesture which is born of warm feelings for the other person and inspires warm feelings in return, and "giving in," in grudging, unconscious anger, which may be born of hate and may breed hate in return.

The same deed can be performed two different ways, or the same words uttered in a different tone, and the very way this is done tells the difference between love and hate.

A man may say, "Please be quiet," to his wife when she talks too loudly while they are watching a movie, disturbing him and others. He may utter this angrily, unclasping his hand from hers, moving to the other side of his seat, and giving her a look of repugnance, and she will feel he hates her.

Or he can say, "Please be quiet," in such a tone that his wife will feel his affection in spite of the words. This is not to say he need be tender and loving every moment of the live-long day, but during important moments, when anger might flash as a response to anger, he should be aware of the effect he is creating.

In the same fashion, "I love you," can be uttered by rote, out of a feeling that it is expected, and love then becomes a mechanical thing. Or the words, "I love you," can breathe fire and tenderness, part of body and soul.

One way in which sexual fear appears in disguised form is through the inhibitions of some brides about undressing in front of their new husbands. Despite the apparent equality of freedom in which boys and girls are brought up, significant differences do exist. Boys are accustomed to undress publicly in locker rooms whereas girls often undress in private cubicles. Thus some girls are not accustomed to dress and undress even in front of members of their own sex, let alone those of the opposite sex.

The Missing Words in the Marriage Manuals

Another problem may arise out of the difficulty some have, even those with previous sexual experience, in communicating their wishes and needs to the other. The bride may not realize that her husband, who appears so manly and confident, may be shy and fearful as to how well he will acquit himself sexually. She may want to understand more about his needs but think it unladylike to ask any questions and this may add to any discomfort she already feels. He, on the other hand, may be too embarrassed to ask questions as to how their adjustment is proceeding because he has not learned to speak openly about his emotions.

Unfortunately, even today some brides cling to the old wives' tale that the first sexual experience will be painful to a woman. The anxiety created by such a fear often causes pain which otherwise would not have existed. Sometimes, too, this fear is inhibiting to the man because of his wish to avoid hurting his bride.

Another peril of the honeymoon period is created by efforts to anticipate and prevent the sexual problems that may arise in marriage by reading all about them before the marriage. Some men and women devour marriage manuals as though they were bibles on how to behave in bed. Such avid readers know their theoretical sex, they are able to discourse learnedly on all the correct techniques, but unfortunately they lack the one essential of satisfying sex—a tender, loving feeling for each other. They engage in sex not so much for pleasure as to prove they have the power to carry out everything mentioned in the manual. A "do or die" attitude about sex does not help promote pleasure.

The happy honeymooner gets enjoyment out of giving from the richness of his own heart, and instructions for this cannot be found on any printed page. It is not a question of "I'll give you and then you give me." A love relationship usually does not thrive on bargaining.

Ideally, there is little competition in love unless it be competition to see who can contribute most in understanding and affection to the other. Instead of jealously sitting back and keeping "book" on how much pleasure one receives from the other, on the happy honeymoon each one strives to give pleasure to the other. He starts to put someone else first, not only because he knows this is a better way of getting along, but because he truly wants to give up part of his narrow selfishness.

Sometimes, even during the honeymoon, a man and woman may start to doubt whether they will make a go of the marriage, to fear that they will not be able to adjust to each other, although they may remain married for years before they finally decide to part.

One woman confessed, after living three years with a husband she finally divorced, "I knew when we were on our honeymoon that we would never be happy. I had built up tremendous illusions about him, none of which were true. The first week I was bored silly—I could predict every word he was going to say. But I stuck it out three years to give it a chance, knowing all the time we would never succeed."

Subtle signs exist, clearly perceptible to both, as to whether their choice has been wise. There may be mixed feelings, for there usually are, but the feelings that predominate give the clue, whether they are ones primarily of tenderness and love or anxiety and hatred.

The honeymoon that is happy ends on the note that it has been a time for only the merest exploration of the other person, sexually and in all other ways. It is but the beginning of a joint venture, one that will contain much joy, much pleasure, and some heartbreak, some sorrow. For these are all part of life, and if there is pleasure, there will also be pain.

Yet stormy honeymoons may still lead to successful marriages. The human capacity to adapt to many kinds of situations is almost infinite. Just as man is able to live at the frigid

North Pole and the torrid equator, and probably someday on the moon, so may he live with a wide variety of mates, given the will and the realization that perfect understanding and ever loving attention are the product not of life but of the fervid imagination of trade writers for True Confession magazines. Marriage is a human institution subject to the frailties of human beings.

3 AFTER THE "TINSEL WEEKS"

As the honeymoon fades into memory, each partner is faced with the serious task of living in intimacy with someone else, keeping his own individuality, yet at the same time contributing his share toward carving out happiness for two. No longer does the romantic fantasy of courtship and honeymoon reign. The reality of day-to-day living sets in with a vengeance.

A degree of disillusionment occurs in almost every marriage once it begins in earnest. If the disenchantment is not too disastrous, the marriage will survive. If the disillusionment is too devastating, the marriage may fail.

What determines the degree of disillusionment? It is caused chiefly by the number of illusions one has about the self, the loved one, and marriage, all of which influence the extent to which conflicts emerge.

Any deep conflict existing before marriage may become highly intensified afterward. Marriage often magnifies all our inner difficulties. The mature person expects it to do so, and sets about tackling the solution of problems as best he can.

Anyone who expects married life to be easy is engulfed by formidable fantasy. Those who scream loudest that their lives *must* be easy are, we may be sure, protesting against the feeling that their psychic lives are very hard; they may not make good risks as marriage partners. Those who quietly accept the fact that life is difficult have come to terms with their inner wish for a fantasy life of effortless ease, one in which they take no responsibility.

Furnishing a House Is Not Always Fun

Conflicts that may exist within often quickly become evident in one of the first practical problems to be faced, the furnishing of a home. Traditionally, the woman is responsible, although sometimes she asks her husband his preference and, in some cases, depends almost completely on his help. Some wives ignore their husband's tastes, either at his request or because they want everything done their way alone.

A woman's personality traits will often be shown in how she furnishes her home. If she is indecisive and uncertain, this will show in the way she goes about selecting its furnishings. She will have no conviction about what she really wants. The selection of every ashtray, every picture on the wall, becomes as dramatic a production as if it were the choice for an elaborate Broadway stage setting.

Or she may engage in endless exchange, never sure of her selection. Some wives redecorate their homes each year, like birds busy with their seasonal nest-building drive. Some women do so because they like a yearly change of scenery in the rooms where they live, others because they are never satisfied with their choice.

The opposite extreme is the wife who does not care and is casual about what she buys as furnishings. This kind of home usually looks haphazard and inharmonious as if there were no planning, no attempt to have a unified color scheme or blending of furniture.

How a home looks also betrays the woman's feelings about herself. A house bursting with flounces and flowered chintz, even unto the husband's study, bespeaks a woman who must flaunt her femininity. She may actually have many masculine feelings, the décor she creates being an attempted denial of such feelings. On the other hand, a very austere home without a sign of femininity, not even a perfume bottle on the bureau, may tell of her fear of being feminine and an underlying belief in the desirability of being masculine.

Usually, although not always, the wife is far more interested in decorating the house than the husband who, as a rule, says, "Get anything you want, dear." This may infuriate an insecure wife if she construes it as meaning he does not care about the home or her or the marriage. One husband told his wife, "As far as I'm concerned, we can furnish the apartment with an army cot and a couple of boxes to sit on." She burst into tears and wailed, "You don't love me!"

The Homogenized Home

It is pathetic that so many homes in America seem to lack taste and character. House after house stands furnished in the same fashion. We tend to be a nation of homogenized homes. Often you cannot tell the difference between houses from their exteriors, and you can tell even less from their interiors. You could shuffle parlor or bedroom from one house to the next without much visible change.

One of the psychological causes of this sameness is that we are often afraid to call attention to ourselves. We carefully submerge all our individuality and try to fade quietly into the background, making ourselves as much like our neighbor as possible. This is an expression of the fear of exhibitionism which we all have to some degree. It often springs from the early years when we were punished if we exhibited our bodies. Then, when we went to school, we were condemned if we showed too much intelligence or too much stupidity, if we were in any way above or below the average.

A certain amount of conformity is necessary and proper, for rebels are among the unhappiest of souls, but not conformity to the point where spirit and taste are dulled as they seem to be when one looks into the average American home. Most of them are devoid of such personal touches as unusual color schemes on the walls, or pictures chosen to taste painted by the occupants or their friends, which may not exactly rival Rembrandt or Renoir but give the home a spark of originality.

Although we are restricted, unless we build our own, to the furniture available on the market, there exists enough of it in good taste to provide for a fair range of selection in style and substance. But the one who selects must have confidence in his own feelings so he can furnish a home that reflects his personality. There will be little harmony and unity in the furnishings if he does not trust his own feelings.

A Root of Evil Feelings

The problem of budgeting is one that may touch off some of the deepest of emotional conflicts as husband and wife jointly decide how to spend the dollars earned. Much can be learned of a person's feelings about himself and others by his attitude toward money.

Sometimes a wife is amazed that a husband who seemed so generous during courtship turns out to be a suburban Scrooge. Perhaps he will still tip as generously as before, carelessly throwing bills at waiters, but he demands that she account for every penny of a too-small household allowance.

One popular notion is that of the man toiling away and tending to be stingy with his hard-earned dollars, and the woman grasping and scheming to get every last cent out of him. Like all stereotypes this is a distorted view of most couples, yet contains a kernel of truth for some. The lie is completely given it, of course, in those families where women work, and today about one-half of all married women are working wives.

Conflicts over money may be caused by both real and unreal problems. It is reality that money, to civilized man, holds the same meaning as food and shelter to primitive man. It determines whether he survives. Money is a matter of life and death in our society, particularly for those raised by parents who endured the depression years in poverty and seem to possess a desperate thrift unknown to those who blithely mortgage themselves to credit firms for house, furniture, and car.

Money also serves as a great focal point for competitiveness, for he who controls the purse strings controls the family. The struggle for money is the struggle for the possession of the potent instrument that paves the way for the buying of coveted things that bring comfort and prestige.

While the cliché that money can't buy happiness is still true, at least it can provide professional help toward better adjustment and greater content than would be possible without it.

To Spend or Not To Spend

A variety of conflicts cluster around the spending of money. One of them is hoarding, or miserliness, shown by the man or woman who holds onto money for the pure gratification of retaining it and for the hostile pleasure of not giving when asked. Such a man or woman is apt to fly into a fury when his mate spends a dollar, even when the spending is for a useful purpose.

One husband, who presents a charming and friendly personality to the world, checks every item his wife buys in the supermarket and becomes enraged if he thinks she pays too much for anything. Before they purchase an article of clothing, they indulge in a tremendous amount of comparison shopping. Once they walked across Manhattan to buy a shirt because it was cheaper than those advertised in any other store. They intended to take the bus back, but it happened to be the day a bus strike started and they were forced to hail a taxi. The husband was furious because he then lost money on the deal.

This same man makes it his business to go shopping with his wife whenever he can find the time. He would actually like to do the shopping himself, but it is too painful for him to spend the money, so he accompanies her and she commits the sin of spending for which he can then berate her.

Hoarders are frequently constipated physiologically as well as financially and emotionally, and, as might be expected, this attitude may carry over also into their sexual lives. The man mentioned above did not seek sexual intimacy often because this, too, involved an expenditure, one of emotional energy. His wife felt she practically had to rape him if she wanted sex. He had trouble giving, even when he could receive pleasure in return.

Opposite from the hoarder is the profligate with his desperate desire to spend whether it is justified or not. A woman who had been to several doctors consulted one who set a rather high fee saying, "I'll be glad to send you to someone else if it's too high."

"Oh, no," she assured him, with a satisfied smile, "I want the very best."

This woman lived in a small two-room apartment with her husband and two children, but insisted on buying the most expensive furniture and household articles. Although she could have purchased these items at a discount through her husband's business connections, she made it a point never to do so. In addition, she refurnished her entire apartment at frequent intervals.

As a child this woman would steal from her mother's purse whenever they had a fight. As an adult, in a sense she was continuing to steal from her husband who, in part, represented her mother. Thus spending was an act of hostility, a way of trying to bankrupt her husband and render him impotent financially.

Women who try to get a man to spend a lot of money during courtship show the same hostility. One young woman made a date to go to a party with a man who was interested in her. First she kept him waiting two hours while she dressed, in itself a sign of hostility, and then she insisted that they stop at several restaurants for drinks on the way to the party. The restaurants were chosen solely because they were expensive, for they were neither convenient nor particularly attractive.

Equally as hostile may be the woman who will not permit a man to spend any money on her, as though to deny his ability to do even this much for her. She is cutting him down to size, as the expression goes, saying in effect, "I am just as good as you," and refusing to accept her role as a woman. She may also be saying, "If you do something for me, then I will owe you something in return and I don't want to owe anyone anything. I want to be in control."

This applies also to women who cannot allow men to open doors for them, or light cigarettes, or perform any of the other amenities which our culture expects from the man. These women, perhaps, are looking for the extinct caveman who had no manners and little respect for the feminine sex.

Such women, when they marry, may find it difficult to appreciate their husbands' accomplishments and may have an unfortunate effect on his career because they refuse to enjoy the trophies he brings home from the financial hunt. Men often thrive on the stimulation of their wives' admiration and acceptance. It helps them to perform adequately.

There is also the husband who discourages his wife from being feminine. Any show of dependence on her part arouses anxiety in him, for he does not feel strong enough to accept her femininity. He wants to lean on her and resents any attempt on her part to be dependent on him.

Some slide into financial disaster because of a compulsion to spend. They try to control their spending sprees by budgeting, by putting part of their salary in the bank immediately upon receiving it, but nothing seems to work. Money pours through their hands like rain on an arid desert, leaving no impression.

One man with a wife and three children would start home with his weekly salary which was needed for rent and food, but then stop off at a bridge club. Although an expert card player, on occasion he would manage to lose not only his salary but go into debt as well. He would also make impulsive, rash purchases so that, while living in what was little better than a slum apartment, at one time he owned three cars and a motorboat.

Neither he nor his wife had learned the importance of controls. As one would guess, along with his inability to manage his finances went a general lack of emotional control. Sometimes he and his wife appeared to love each other, but at other times they would give vent to such violent outbursts of rage that on several occasions the police arrived, summoned by horrified neighbors who were afraid that a murder was being committed.

The Importance of Children

During the first year of marriage, the question of having children will often arise. The custom of marriage evolved out of the need to protect the family, devised so the man would remain with the woman and provide for her economically through the years during which she nurtured and raised children. Therefore, since one of the main purposes of marriage is to produce children and insure the continuation of the race, if either husband or wife is adamantly opposed to having them, this is a matter that should be investigated further psychologically because the frustration of the parental drive of one mate by the other can be a source of serious difficulty.

Differing Sexual Needs

Also during the first months of marriage, conflicts over sexual intimacy may become apparent. Each may discover that the other's needs are quite different from his own. Usually the man desires sexual intimacy more often, although some experts estimate that about one-third of those who complain of their partner's lack of sexual interest are women.

One woman, after she had been married six months, became unhappy over her husband's mild sexual interest in her. She wondered whether, under such circumstances, it would be wrong for her to find a lover to make up for the deficit. If she had a lover, she thought, she could be a more pleasant wife because she then would not be so irritable,

jumpy, and combative and so resentful of her husband's failure to show sufficient romantic interest in her.

This would, of course, be no solution since the complications bound to arise from such a situation would be even
more difficult to solve. Her husband was fanatically possessive and jealous, as such men are apt to be. Because, since
they are well aware of their wife's lack of fulfillment, they are
constantly fearful, or perhaps even expect that she will seek
elsewhere the gratification they deny her.

We could wonder why this woman picked such a man. She
had been married before and her first husband made excessive
sexual demands on her which she found intolerable. Her
deep dissatisfaction with her lot as a woman expressed itself
in her choice of a mate—one husband was damned because
he did, the other because he didn't.

She had conflicts within herself which she would have to
face before she would be able to live happily with anyone, no
matter how many husbands she tried. The Tommy Manvilles
of the world, both masculine and feminine, solve nothing
except perhaps a more equitable distribution of their fortunes
as they dole them out to "ex's."

Our feelings about sexuality are the most sensitive of all
feelings because we spend so much of our energy as we grow
up denying them or repressing them. When finally, in marriage, we are given permission to express sexuality, it may take
a bit of practice to become comfortable within ourselves. At
times a mate may unknowingly contribute an added difficulty.
For instance, even with today's frank advertising, there are
women and men who do not pay enough attention to making
themselves hygienically or esthetically pleasing to their partners.

"How in Hades do you get romantic with a woman who
looks as though she's wired for sound, with huge, ugly metal

curlers poking out of her head and her face smeared with hog grease?" complained one husband.

Women are more apt to be offended by strong smells such as mouth, underarm, or cigar odors. The sense of smell plays a powerful part in arousing sexual desire in civilized man, as it did in primitive societies, and does in the animal kingdom. Perfumes and after-shave lotions stand as the modern sub-stitutes for the love philter and the aphrodisiac, as our ad-vertisements make flagrantly clear—the stoical man takes one whiff of the woman's perfume and promptly hurls aside his violin to embrace her violently against the grand piano.

No Right or Wrong Time for Sex

The spontaneity of the courtship days may become suffocated in marriage unless it is deliberately sustained. It is desirable that as much spontaneity as possible be preserved, for sex seems to be far more enjoyable when it is spontaneous.

Some try to regulate their sexual intimacy in a set pat-tern, such as indulging on week ends, or only at night. One woman would permit intercourse with her husband only on the night he handed her his weekly salary—he was fortunate he was not paid monthly.

Quite a different spirit was shown by another wife as she and her husband, married two years, were walking along the sands of a deserted beach one night. They looked at each other, felt they wanted to make love under the stars with the surf pounding away in front of them. It proved one of the most unforgettable experiences of their early married life.

Another woman might have deprived herself and her hus-band of both the delightful experience and the cherished memory, the stuff of which happy marriages are built. Such a woman might have been afraid someone would stumble by and discover them, or that the sand would be uncomfortable, or scoffed at the idea of a couple married two years making love in such an unconventional place.

True, making love should be conducted in private but there was little danger in this instance that anyone would pass by, or at least anyone other than another couple with similar feelings, who would quickly retreat to their own privacy.

A Room of Their Own

The importance of privacy in love-making is recognized today by many parents who realize the danger of engaging in sexual intimacy while a child sleeps in the same room. The risk of the child waking and becoming frightened by a scene he can only interpret as violence is too great to be taken in terms of his future emotional life.

Babies are extremely aware of everything that goes on around them, although they cannot interpret it rationally. One couple realized that their baby woke up and cried every time they started to embrace each other at night and moved his crib to another room, thus improving conditions for both their own and their child's emotional security.

The study of a number of our murderers and delinquents shows that, as babies, they often slept in the same room as their parents. This is not to say that awareness of their parents' love-making alone caused them to be unable to control their violence in later life, but only that it is difficult enough for a child to learn to control his impulses without thrusting added hazards in his way.

When we blame crime and delinquency on poor economic conditions, we might take into account that those very conditions also contribute to emotional ill health in that parents and children are forced to live in abnormal closeness where the children have no chance to escape knowledge of what goes on sexually between their parents. They are inevitably over-stimulated by what they see and hear and sense.

It may take a while for newly married couples to adjust sexually and in other ways, but those able to love tend to show patience and understanding toward themselves and their mates. They accept the months following the honey-moon as marking their first mutual encounter with reality. Each one welcomes the chance to know the other better, to take responsibility for his own conflicts, and to enjoy the many moments of delight that come only out of being shared with someone beloved.

4   *MARRIAGE AS A VENDETTA*

All too many marriages end, either with a bang or a whimper, in divorce court. The percentage increases constantly—since the turn of the century the number of divorces in this country has more than tripled. Our nation has the highest divorce rate in the world, with one divorce to every three marriages.

Hundreds of thousands of other couples separate permanently without going to the trouble of a formal divorce, chiefly those who cannot afford it. Many a husband leaves home to go down to the corner store for a loaf of bread or sets out for a walk and never returns, à la Gauguin. Or perhaps husband and wife agree to separate without a divorce, believing they will not marry again. Countless men and women live this way, not married in any sense of the word, but not divorced either.

Then there are thousands of other married couples who live together in the climate of a cold war, not divorced, not separated. They exist from day to day barely tolerating each other, smoldering with ill-concealed rage. They stay enmeshed in their web of discontent, wanting to break away but not knowing how, or perhaps not daring to make the try, figuring that half a loaf of love is better than none.

They are angry because the one relationship in which they invested so many of their hopes turned out to be not nearly so dazzling as they dreamed it would be. They now live with someone not out of love but more out of hate, tied together by knots of guilt, feeling incapable of supplying a warmth they would like to share.

Their hatred erupts in many ways, for hate will not remain concealed for long. It may show itself in the most civilized manner, such as the verbal slaughter of one's mate. Or it may be disguised as an overzealous desire to please. Or it may exude an excessive protectiveness. Or it may be spewed out as an eternal "no" to everything the other suggests. Or it may sputter forth in constant bickering.

"Why do you always put my shirts in the drawer with the collars to the back when I've asked you so often to put them the other way?" an irritated husband will demand. It is hostile of his wife to continue doing this in the face of his constant request and he returns the hostility, a vicious circle of getting even.

"Stop scattering ashes in all of the ashtrays and stick to one," a wife will nag her husband. It is hostile of the husband to ignore her request and for her to make an issue of the ashtrays. Both the acts and the nagging they bring forth show the underlying anger.

Psychological Warfare on the Home Front

One subtle way of expressing hostility has, alas, been offered by modern psychology. Its terms and theories are misused by couples who employ as epithets and insults words which the psychiatrist uses carefully and dispassionately purely for descriptive or diagnostic purposes.

For instance, a psychiatrist considers the description "neurotic" to be no more indication of moral depravity than the general practitioner speaking of a virus. Yet husbands and wives will sneer at each other for being "neurotic" or, when particularly angered, as "psychotic."

After reading a book on psychology one husband boasted, "Instead of referring to my wife as a shrew, I now call her a psychoneurotic." He had not, of course, changed his attitude toward her one whit, although he changed the epithet.

"You're too introverted—you should get outside of yourself more," one wife told her husband.

"The trouble with you is that you're too attached to your mother," another snapped at her husband.

You cannot maintain a good sexual relationship with anyone and at the same time analyze his behavior, telling him what is wrong with him. Even in psychoanalysis, with the help of an analyst over a long period of time, it is difficult to accept a critical look at the self. You cannot constantly criticize or appear to criticize someone from whom you wish desire and tenderness—you can hardly slug someone in the psyche and expect him to respond with love.

Analysis and criticism of a mate's behavior are used to mask one's own hostility. They are a very effective defense against having to face one's own feelings and failings.

Husband and wife should feel free to discuss whatever disturbs them but preferably not in the form of a direct attack upon each other. The surest way to weaken affection is to tell someone what is wrong with him too often. This is as destructive to love as taking an ax to a butterfly. After the first, "You don't seem at ease with people—where's your self-confidence?" or "Can't you buy more attractive hats?" or "Did you have to be so nasty tonight in front of guests?" uttered in critical, disparaging tone, the war is on.

Some are well aware of the hatred in which they live. One man who kept complaining of his wife's nagging was asked by a friend, "Why don't you leave her if she's so awful?"

"Where else could I find such a worthy antagonist?" he replied, confessing that his purpose in getting married was to have someone with whom to fight.

Much of life for those who live in hatred is concerned with who is "right." This is a carry-over from childhood, for children scream at each other, "I'm right—you're wrong!" and much of childhood is a battle to be "right." But when this same determination is shown by partners in a marriage, it is no help in maintaining a good relationship.

There is, of course, no "right" or "wrong." Each is "right" in terms of his life and how he sees the world and "wrong" in that he is not considering the other's wishes and feelings. If you love someone, there will be times he is wrong and you are right but it will not matter. For love is not founded on who is right and who is wrong but solely on whether we think the other lovable enough, and respect him enough, to go along with his wishes even if we do not agree with them. Some try to offer tenderness, affection, and admiration even when they may disagree.

They Suffer To Conquer

One of the most difficult expressions of hostility with which to deal is that of depression, illness, and suffering. This is often used as veiled attack by those who take to chronic complaint as a way of getting rid of a hatred they will not face.

One woman, known to her friends and relatives as "poor, sick Helen," constantly complains of headaches, heart palpitations, and other internal pains, always blaming her husband for causing them. She has succeeded in turning her two children and her friends against this "brute of a man," although she never attacks him directly. He, too, accepts her illness as real and suffers pangs of guilt with no possibility of fighting off her assault since one cannot be angry with a sick person.

Such women erroneously believe their suffering will bring them love. They claim the love of their husband and children on the grounds that they earn it by their privations and illness. They have believed, from childhood on, that they were deprived of love, affection, and attention except when they were in pain or suffering. It is a sad fact that some mothers do give their greatest attention to a child when he is sick, their concern showing chiefly at a time of illness. The child who is always sick may be trying to seek love in the only way he knows how to get it, which is then what he also does as an adult, although it comes across to those with whom he lives as hostility, rather than a pathetic plea for love.

Another way of showing hostility is to discuss past romances, even a past marriage. Such relationships should be accepted, if they existed, but not hauled out and flung in a mate's face as they are examined in minute detail and comparisons, spoken or unspoken, made.

One husband kept reminding his wife about a woman with whom he once lived. "Sue wouldn't have done it this way," he would say. Or he would recall wistfully, "Sue had such a sweet disposition," implying his wife was a tyrant. Such remarks may mask deep hostility and cannot help but arouse hostility in the mate even though he or she may smile politely and appear to be untroubled.

The "Loving" Competitors

Competition, when it is extreme, can be detrimental to a marriage. Sometimes it is obvious, sometimes buried deep beneath layers of apparent acceptance of the achievements of the mate with no expressed wish to compete. The competition may take many forms—in work, in hobbies, in sports, with children, with friends and relatives

There may even be competition to see who suffers the most. At a cocktail party the hostess greeted her guests in a charming, well-poised manner, apologizing for the absence of her husband who was still at work but expected momentarily. When he walked in twenty minutes later, she asked gaily, "How are you, darling?"

"Terrible," he said tonelessly. "I had a tough day at the office."

Immediately her voice and manner changed. She retorted, "*You* feel terrible? You ought to know what I've been through getting ready for this party with a ghastly headache." For the next fifteen minutes the guests were treated to a discussion as to who had suffered more that day, husband at office or wife at home. It appeared a draw.

A certain amount of competition is natural, necessary for each of us to survive, but perhaps not to the degree to which most of us are subjected, starting early in life and continuing thereafter. A youngster in the fourth grade was recently asked by a visitor, "How are you doing in school?" one of those inane questions adults usually put to children, not knowing what to say, and probably the one subject the child likes least to talk about.

"Pretty good," said the boy unhappily.

"Getting high marks?" asked the adult.

"They're all right," he replied. Then he added in a puzzled tone, "The only thing I'm not doing so well in is 'Cooperation.' The teacher says I'm not cooperating as good as the other kids."

The adult grimaced at the ludicrousness of asking children to compete to see who was the most cooperative.

Parents sometimes intensify a child's competitive spirit. Some peck at their children with such persistent queries as, "Did you get the highest marks in your class this month?" The child soon feels the important thing is not the enjoyment of learning but the defeat of all his classmates scholastically. He also feels his parents do not care for him as a person but only because he is the academic conqueror of his classmates.

Within the home parents sometimes play one child against the other. When a child misbehaves they snap, "Why can't you be as good as your brother?" or when his marks are not as high as they wish, "Why aren't you as smart as your sister?" Enough natural hostility exists among brothers and sisters, or brothers and brothers, or sisters and sisters, without their needing any parental encouragement to compete. These are often the same parents who, at any display of anger between their children, will rebuke them, saying they are supposed to love each other.

One mother was describing how popular her older son had become. "Everyone in school loves him, even the teachers," she told a friend enthusiastically.

Whereupon her younger son looked at her and said emphatically, "I don't like him."

She replied casually, with an awareness all too few mothers possess, "You're not supposed to—you're his brother."

Sometimes a parent will favor one child over the other to such a degree that the unfavored child either must compete excessively (feeling it is in vain but nonetheless that he must keep trying) or gives up in despair, refusing to compete at all. One of the saddest stories on record is told about the late Robert Benchley by his son, Nathaniel, in the latter's book, *Robert Benchley: A Biography*. When Benchley *père* was a young man, his older brother, sent overseas in World War I, was killed in battle.

When she received the tragic news, his mother, who had adored her oldest son, said bitterly to the younger Benchley, "Why couldn't it have been you?"

No wonder Benchley had to laugh ironically at life.

Some authorities believe that if a parent is able to love, he will be able to give love to all his children. If he is not able to love, he will be able to give love to none of them. Although he may appear to love one child more than the other, this is a feeling that arises out of his needs, not out of love for the child, and the child who seems to be overloved will be just as unhappy as the child who is openly hated. Parents cannot feel the same toward every child, for it is impossible to love all children in the same way, but in a reasonably healthy atmosphere children learn to accept such differences as a fact of life.

A child may be used as a pawn if parents compete to win his love. "Look at all I've done for you," says a mother, implying the father has done nothing. Or she may say this openly when the child comes to her asking for a favor and she replies, "Why don't you go to your father? He does little enough for you," implying the father does not love the child as much as she does. Children should be brought up to feel love and respect for both parents but they find it difficult to do this if one parent continually tears down the other in the presence of the children.

Some parents do things for a child out of hatred for what their own parents did to them. They may indulge a child because they felt deprived by their parents. This is an unhappy motive, for it does not put the child first, nor does it indicate any understanding of his needs. One mother allowed her daughter to go untrained in toilet functions for three years because she had resented so deeply her very early toilet training. The child would be far happier today if she had been toilet trained at a normal period in her life, learning the control that all of us must learn.

In much of the world's activities, the emphasis is not on enjoyment but on defeating the other fellow. This is certainly true of sports. In almost all spheres of life, we are expected to compete but then suddenly when we marry, this highly developed spirit of competition is magically supposed to stop, for one does not compete with his beloved. Unfortunately, in some instances the early lessons have been too well learned and competition will proceed full speed ahead and insidiously corrode the marriage.

Competition may appear in many subtle forms. The battles which take place between parents as to who will do the dishes or put the children to bed is competition, either for the assumption of, or to evade, responsibility. A wife may be competing with her husband when he starts to tell a joke and she groans, "Not that old chestnut again!" Perhaps she interrupts, to tell the story in her own way, or if she is more sophisticated about the attack, she will ring the bell for the maid to bring in dessert just as he reaches the punch line.

Some women are inwardly furious at being female, one of their most fervent unconscious wishes being that they had been born a man, mistakenly believing this would bring them greater freedom and pleasure. They spend the better (or worst) part of their lives competing with men; and when they marry, the husband bears the brunt of their competitive, envious spirit.

They usually choose men whose neurotic needs fit theirs, men who need to be controlled, who may rant openly against the domination but who, nonetheless, seek this kind of woman. For them it is the lesser of two evils, living alone being the other, although choice on this basis does not make for a happy marriage.

Men, too, may compete with wives who are successful

career women, masking their envy with admiration but unable to keep their competitive drive from breaking out every so often in angry ways, such as criticism or disparagement.

The spirit of competition between the sexes has not been lessened by recent social changes. Fifty or sixty years ago it was taken for granted that the man was breadwinner and head of the household. The masculine and feminine roles were clearly defined and no woman dreamed of competing with her husband in the world of work. But now women may hold all kinds of jobs if they so desire, openly competing with men with the full approval of society.

A Frenchwoman, when asked about the difference between American and French families, said, "We women in France do not have to compete because we have been equal for so long. Your American women are losing their femininity in their effort to assert their equality." She was, of course, speaking of the urban Frenchwoman, not the farm woman.

Some couples live together in hatred that may range from an intense active disgust to a complete ignoring of each other. There are those who fight angrily all the time and those who speak not a word in their wrath, using silence as a weapon.

When Looks Would Kill

Feeling and expression of anger is a natural human function. But it is preferable to know if we hate for a real reason or if we hate for a fancied wrong. It is preferable to know whether we are righteously angry or unable to tolerate normal frustration, if our hatred of others may not be a projection of self-hatred, serving only to eat away at our acceptance of ourselves and those with whom we are involved.

If we are really able to understand what causes our anger before it builds up, we can often keep from exploding. If we know the true target of our wrath, we realize we may be gripped by an unreasonable fury and therefore may be able to exercise enough control not to hurl it at those we love.

The ultimate in hatred is the desire to kill, which one may or may not recognize as the underlying feeling. Civilization teaches us to disguise this primitive feeling in many ways, some of which we use to deceive ourselves.

One man was aware how miserably he and his wife got along although he tried in every way to please her. One day he asked her, "What's the matter? Why can't we act friendly toward each other?"

"I'm afraid of you," she said. "I feel you want to kill me."

"Kill you?" he said in bewilderment. "I do all I can to please you."

"Yes, but you often look at me as though you wish I were dead," she said.

He had tried hard to please his wife just as during his earlier life he had tried to please his mother. He had never dared express anger toward his beloved mother, as he had never expressed it toward his wife. Instead, he subjected her to black, sullen looks that told her of his hatred more clearly than any words. But he could truthfully say that never a harsh word had escaped his lips and delude himself that he felt no hatred in his heart.

One woman, whose outstanding expression was a zombie-like smile, boasted, "I never heard my mother and father raise their voices to each other." Her father was a minister, her mother came from a minister's family, and all fury was submerged, expressed only in her father's too-soft voice and her mother's stoic migraine smile. Some who have harbored a tremendous rage they have dammed up over the years can hardly talk at all, or speak only in a whisper, or find it difficult to speak in front of strangers.

Feelings Speak Louder than Words

In marriage it is helpful to feel free to express all feelings including anger. Often accepting and putting such feelings into words prevents us from acting on them. If one fears that his murderous rages will explode into action, he may need professional help.

When we read in our newspapers about a man who suddenly bursts into an apparently inexplicable mad rage killing several people, his neighbors often describe him as a kind, quiet, soft-spoken individual. Perhaps if he had been able to vent some of his anger in words, he would have been able to prevent the fatal explosion.

If one lives in continuous angry silence with a mate, he should examine carefully the reasons why. Some who are afraid of their anger will go so far as to break up the marriage rather than express what they consider hostile feelings. It is a mistaken notion that we must be supremely understanding and tolerant at all times. This is beyond the ken of human beings as we know them today. Yet, to become the slightest bit upset in the sight of someone we think we are supposed to love is considered by some to be as great a sin as cannibalism.

An inimical thought when expressed, is often found to be based on misunderstanding. One woman said to her husband, "I have a feeling you never could express tenderness before you met me."

He was silent.

In a hurt tone she said, "Oh! Now you're angry at me."

"No, I'm not," he said thoughtfully. "I'm just looking inward to know how I really feel."

She realized she had mistaken his silence for anger when he was only trying to be truthful.

Either of the two extremes, the suppression of all emotion or overindulging in the expression of feelings, is better avoided if one wishes to live a reasonably peaceful existence. A middle course should be steered, if possible, between the Gary Cooper complex, in which the display of great emotion is limited to the clenching of teeth or the movement of a muscle of the ear, and the endless dramatic emoting which some cannot halt.

Why Talking It Out Helps

Hidden anger is frightening both to the self and others. It is less frightening if, on occasion, we are able to show anger to ourselves and our mate. If someone accepts us, they accept the fact there will be times when we are angry and it may have little or nothing to do with them.

One man who had taken a young woman out several times, called one night to break a date. "I feel angry so I better go straight home," he said. "I'm in no mood to cheer you up."

"You're not required to be Pollyanna," she said. "Why don't you just come over to be with me and tell me what's troubling you?"

He took a taxi to her apartment and, after a few quiet drinks and discussion of problems at the office that upset him, he said, "Thanks for listening. It's good to know I can relax with you and tell you whatever is on my mind."

"I'm glad you feel better," she smiled. "Maybe sometime I'll claim your ear in return."

Sometimes in talking over why we are angry the causes become clearer. A husband may complain about the toughness of the steak at dinner but he is really furious because his wife refused his sexual advances that morning. If the troublesome cards are on the table, the mate who is truly interested in understanding the other cannot help but be moved by the honesty.

For a full relationship it is helpful, too, to say occasionally, "I won't," or "no," but to say it quietly, out of a firm conviction in yourself, not out of anger or to antagonize. Sometimes a mate will welcome the setting of a limit, one he might have liked to impose himself but did not dare.

A wife had been going to the house of one couple for dinner, month after month, because she thought her husband liked them although she found them uninteresting and hostile. One night when he brought home another invitation from this couple, the wife said quietly, "I don't want to go there again. We have little enough time together and I don't see why we should spend it with people who make us anxious."

He looked at her admiringly and said, "I wish I had the guts to have said it first."

The important thing is to know what you feel. You do not necessarily have to express it or act on it. As one woman put it, "Control without denial." It is not easy to have adequate control if the feeling is not faced directly.

Thinking Is Not Doing

Some find it difficult to know what they feel. They fear they will act on the feeling if it becomes conscious, so they repress it. To a certain degree we all must do this to become civilized but we should be aware of the difference between a thought and a deed. The child believes if he thinks a thing it means doing it—the deed is done if he but dreams it.

For instance, some adults feel so guilty at the thought of hating a parent that they quickly bury such a wicked feeling, not daring to admit it is true, but then they easily transfer the

hate to a mate where it seems more appropriate. It is not uncommon for a husband to blame his wife for the very act he
has praised in his mother, or a wife to berate her husband
for the exact words her father may have used to her, and at
which she had beamed.

The mature person is willing to face his feelings, be they
anger, guilt, or jealousy, and accept them, reasonably secure
in the knowledge that he is master of them. He is not afraid
of a momentary flash of feeling that he would like to throttle
his wife as she shows interest in a handsome neighbor, nor is
his wife afraid of a moment of jealousy as her husband praises
his mother's cooking over hers.

Jealousy, too, is a normal human emotion. If one is aware
of jealous feelings when they occur and accepts them as part
of human nature, he will not take it out on his mate. He will
feel secure enough within himself and with his mate to know
the mate loves him even if she occasionally looks at another
member of the opposite sex.

We often choose as mates those whose needs fit ours and to
blame them when we feel angry is not seeing truth. If there is
constant fighting in a marriage, it solves nothing for each
one to blame the other.

"She's made my life a hell," said one man of a selfish,
querulous wife.

"*You* picked her," said his friend.

Divorce Rarely Helps

Those who divorce and try again often find that although the
face of wife or husband has changed, the conflicts remain the
same. The sad truth is they frequently pick the same type of
mate and would continue to do so even though they tried
twenty times. Although on the surface the choice may seem

different, fundamentally it is often much the same as the first one. If a person is unhappy, the problems frequently lie within him and change of mate does not affect them. It would be a far wiser solution if he tried, after the first touch of trouble, to take an honest look at himself.

While it is important to recognize feelings of anger and occasionally to express them, if too much anger explodes between husband and wife in quantity and quality, it does not take a Freud to know they are obviously out to destroy each other psychologically. If too great a destructiveness has taken place between a couple, expert help may be needed and even then sometimes the break is too deep and they part, temporarily or permanently.

A helpful attitude in a marriage is one of "Your enemy shall be my enemy," not *"You* are my enemy." A wife who snaps at a husband who has lost a business deal, "You handled it all wrong!" or "Didn't you know enough not to go into it in the first place?" instead of trying to see it from his point of view, is often felt by him to be siding with his enemy.

When a husband comes home from the office irritable and worried, it will ease the tension if his wife helps him feel he is at least king in his home and gives him the solace of expressing himself to an understanding listener rather than saying, as one wife did, "The hell with him. He's in a bad mood and I'm not going to put up with such nonsense." An understanding wife would let her husband talk out his troubles, realizing he has fears as does everyone. The wife who cannot do this, but always puts her own feelings first, may be caught in her narcissism and, rationalize as she will, she may be unable to comfort her husband when he may need it most.

Where there is intense anger, humor goes out the window and people cannot live comfortably without using their sense of humor a good deal of the time. We are not characters in a modern drama, or rather, caricatures, as portrayed by some playwrights who depict women as vultures and men as castrated creatures, unrelieved by any sense of humor about themselves. We need humor. It is indispensable in keeping things in true perspective and maintaining emotional balance.

One way of fighting awareness of inner hatred is to make of everything a production, to dramatize even the little things. There are those who create a drama out of all they do, whether it is losing a collar button or earring or deciding what movie to see or where to go for dinner. The "production" may be made either over what is dreaded or delightful, both joy and pain distorted out of all relation to what is real. Nothing is quiet pleasure or mild irritation but must be blown up into bigness by an inner fury, as in the world of the child where everything looms as either horrible or wonderful.

Lysistrata Still Lives

One of the weapons with which adversaries in a marriage strike at each other is sex. Some women refuse to engage in sexual intimacy out of their anger at their husbands. One such woman said bitterly to a friend, "I make my husband suffer when I'm angry at him—the more he begs for sex, the louder I say 'no.' "

Such women in their hatred may often be extremely provocative and seductive in order to entice and then refuse. They are examples of the most devastating epithet in the adolescent male's vocabulary to describe a girl who promises everything and gives nothing—a teaser.

There are men who do the same thing out of their fear and hatred of women, arousing the woman and then refusing her gratification. The man who suffers from premature ejaculation is often telling the woman of his hatred or fear of her.

He wants unconsciously to rob her of the pleasure of sexual satisfaction as his revenge.

A little teasing has its place in sexual stimulation but when carried to an extreme and when no gratification follows, it is often a strong sign of hostility to the opposite sex.

Refusal to indulge in sexual intimacy may, however, mean other things, too. One man, lying in bed with his wife, put his arms out to embrace her. As she sometimes did when not in the mood, she disengaged herself none too tenderly. He attempted to make light of this rebuff by saying in a jocular tone, "You know what, darling? Since we get along well except for this difficulty about my sexual demands, why don't I find somebody else just for sex and then I won't get angry at you when you don't want me?"

She countered by asking, "What do you mean we get along well? It only looks that way because I give in to you all the time. I don't get this 'getting along well' bit."

He turned away from her. "You look at everything bitterly because you feel so bitter about yourself," he said angrily.

What started as an attempt at closeness on his part now became a furious fight in which neither held back on mean words and soon they were shrieking at each other, livid with rage.

The husband, as some husbands do, had looked upon his wife's temporary disinterest in his advances as rejection and attack. The wife, feeling inadequate because of her inability to respond sexually every time her husband desired her, feared he would desert her because of her low sexual desire. This fear burst forth full strength when he joked about finding a sexual substitute, and she defended herself by fighting back.

If she had not possessed this deep fear (of her own sexuality, of his leaving her) she might have passed off his facetiously phrased but hostile remark at its surface meaning. She would have merely smiled or entered into the spirit of the moment by countering, "Would you prefer a blonde or brunette?"

He insisted on considering her rejection of his advances as a personal rejection although it had very little to do with him since, on many other occasions, she had been loving and tender in response to his embrace. Some men do not understand that a woman's sexual desire, much more than a man's, may vary at times. Some women find it difficult to be deeply sexually aroused except during their monthly cycle. However, as a rule sexual desire is the result of many factors for civilized human beings, factors that may be both physiological and psychological.

We can understand that fear is sometimes the cause of anger but it is still difficult to live with a fearful, angry person. Some of us can love a person only when we are convinced that we are loved in return. If the one we love is hostile toward us and blames us for all that goes wrong, it becomes hard to hold onto our tender, affectionate feelings.

If too much anger intrudes upon a marriage, the recipient is apt to want to flee. Sometimes those who are consistently angry or uncontrollably angry at times, will seek seriously to understand why they are subject to such wrath. If they are able to achieve a peace within themselves, the marriage usually has a better chance to endure. If they are not, they may lose out on marriage, for anger is not a good companion and certainly has little to do with love except perhaps to gradually destroy it.

Even though at times we may feel anger at those we love the most, if anger is not the essence of the relationship, it has a chance of succeeding.

5 WE MUST BE ONE

The most commonly expressed aim of marriage is that two shall become as one. Some look upon the phrase "joined together," mentioned in the marriage ceremony, as meaning literally joined, not even as far apart as Siamese twins who maintain two separate psychic identities, but are fused as one, physically.

They envision life shared completely, all loneliness ended, all hurts miraculously healed. They feel now they possess someone with whom they can "find" themselves, from whom there will be no separation.

This need to think of two as one stems from a deep fear of separation. An extreme in this feeling was shown by a young wife who complained that she found sexual intimacy painful because she could not stand the separation that followed the joining of her body with her husband's. A devastating fear of the separation that would inevitably ensue each time they made love, destroyed her pleasure in the act of coming together.

Part of this feeling arose from her natural wish to be filled, as a woman, with a child. Obstetricians who are aware of the connection between physical illness and emotional conflicts explain some difficult cases of childbirth as due to the mother's unconscious desire to retain the baby within her because this makes her feel more complete.

Also, part of the young wife's wish for oneness arose from her natural desire to complement her husband. We look to our mate to supply certain aspects missing in ourselves. Thus, the feminine woman needs the masculinity of her husband, and vice versa. Similarly, a shy, quiet woman may seek an outgoing, articulate man who will speak for her, or a very aggressive woman will select a rather passive man. It is from such observations that the commonly expressed notion, "opposites attract" is derived.

The young wife, whose fear of separation was so intense as to destroy her pleasure in sex, needed psychological help to realize that her fear was not normal but a carry-over from an overly close attachment to her mother which she had never faced. When there exists this kind of wish, to remain perpetually close to someone in a bodily sense, it almost always represents the wish as a child to be held close to the body of the parent and snuggled and cuddled.

Marriage Is Not for Children

This same desperate need to cling may also be shown in an emotional sense, as well as physical. Usually the one who clings is unaware of the degree to which he indulges in this parasitic behavior. He does not realize he is draining the other of emotional energy and, at the same time, crippling himself even further.

Possessive clinging may mask a deep fear of standing alone because one feels weak and dependent. It also may hide the fear that the mate will leave for somebody more worthy. One woman tried to hold onto her husband by constantly emphasizing her helplessness. She refused to learn how to make out a check, or perform the simplest repairs around the home, or drive a car, so that her husband was forced to take care of all these duties for her, all the while resenting her lack of independence.

As a child of three, idolized by her parents, this woman had been suddenly deprived of their lavish attention when a younger sister was born. Naturally, the new baby was weak and helpless and the older child unconsciously tried ever after to become the most helpless member of the family in a vain effort to regain the center of attention.

When this woman became a mother herself she acted as if she were the infant and her child the mother, often saying as she dressed the little girl, "See how Mommy takes care of you? When you grow up, you'll take care of Mommy." In lesser degree many parents unconsciously treat their children as though the children should act as good mothers to them.

Only the independent can become interdependent, the happy state for marriage. The one who must perpetuate the dependency of his childhood is not slated to be a thoughtful marriage partner.

The clinging of mother to son, or father to daughter, is an all too well-known tragedy of stunted emotional growth. A bachelor in his mid-thirties visited his mother regularly for Sunday brunch. One Sunday over the eggs and bacon, his mother was, as usual, exhibiting her dependency by asking why he did not come more often, complaining that she never went any place because there was nobody to take her, and asking him to find her a larger apartment, although she was a healthy, vigorous woman, well able to search for one herself.

Finally the son turned to her and said, "Listen to this story,

Mother. 'Once there was a mama bird and three baby birds and they all wanted to go to Europe. The baby birds weren't strong enough to fly all the way across the ocean but they could make it if from time to time they could rest on the mother's back. So they started off on their flight across the Atlantic.

" 'After several hundred miles one of the birds grew tired and perched on his mother's back as she flew along. "Tell me," the mother said to the little one. "When you grow up and I'm old and feeble, will you carry me on your back?"

" 'The little bird said, "Of course, Mama."

" 'Whereupon the mother promptly turned over and let the little bird plummet into the ocean.

" 'Shortly afterwards, the second bird rested on her back. Again she asked the same question. When the little bird replied he would be glad to carry his mother when he grew up, she disposed of him in like fashion.

" 'Finally the third bird was resting on his mother's back. She asked him the question she had put to the other two birds.

"He replied, "No, Mother. When I grow up, I will have little birds of my own to take care of. And while I will try to do all I can for you, my real responsibility will be to my little birds, not to you."

" 'The mother bird smiled happily, the two continued their flight, and reached Europe together.' "

As the son finished this story, his mother sat in silence, staring at her empty coffee cup for several moments. Then she slammed her fist on the table and exclaimed, "Birds are different from people!"

It was no accident her son was a bachelor. A mother who refused to give up her dependency on a grown son might well be one who unconsciously would not wish to see him grow emotionally mature so he could accept a wife and forsake his mother. Some parents need a certain amount of help from children in their old age, but this is quite different from the parent who will not relinquish his child emotionally.

Sometimes in a marriage the partner is unable to accept a mate until he realizes the clinging is not as intense as he thought. One wife, who felt her husband often withdrew from her, was amazed when suddenly she experienced from him a new tenderness and warmth. She could not understand what had made the difference and asked him about it.

At first he was unaware there was a difference, or the reasons for it. Then he realized that his feelings toward her had changed after she had told him about some of her past experiences with men. He saw he was not indispensable to her, whereas previously he had felt tied to her because of what he believed her overwhelming need for him, and he had not dared to permit himself even to think of leaving her, although at times he wished he could. He recognized she was not as dependent on him as he thought and that, should he leave her, she would be able to get along adequately after some sorrow. Now he wished to stay because he genuinely wanted to for his own sake, not only because he felt she needed him.

Mates Cannot Be Parents to Each Other

When either husband or wife feels overly "needed" in the same way a parent is needed to take care of a child, he or she will often resent it. Dependency detracts from his sense of identity, tries to make him into something he cannot be, should not be. We cannot ask our mate to be the parent we had in childhood, or the parent we wished we had.

There is bound to be a little of the parental feeling in every marriage. The more facets there are in a relationship, the richer the relationship. Ideally a woman should be wife, sweetheart, mistress, mother, friend, companion, housekeeper. But if one facet predominates too greatly, to the exclusion of the others, there may be unhappiness. Every man wants a bit of the maternal in his wife but usually not so much that the sweetheart or companion gets lost.

When couples are extremely possessive of each other, frequently although not always, the feelings seesaw between constant quarreling and sickening slavery. When husband and wife have little need to "possess" each other, they are likely to get along more easily.

You cannot fully possess anyone else. You can only be in possession of yourself. The desire to possess another may mean that one is seeking not a mate but a mother. The infant thinks of his mother as his slave, born to do his bidding and fulfill his every wish. When this attitude is carried over excessively into a marriage, it may impair the chance for happiness, for it has little to do with mature love but comes out of childhood yearning for a parent's care and affection.

The Importance of Privacy

Few of us can stand enslavement happily. Most of us have a need for a small world of our own, for a certain amount of privacy in our intellectual, emotional, and physical lives. We are entitled to thoughts and feelings, some pleasant, some unpleasant, that are ours alone, which we need not, and should not, be compelled to share with anyone.

We are also entitled to privacy in our physical functions, which includes the privacy of the bathroom. A fear so strong that it even keeps some from getting married is that they will not be able to retain the privacy for personal functions, which they hold dear. Others are not bothered at all by having this privacy invaded and enjoy, even demand, the sharing of the bathroom at times with their mate. But if one feels he must have this privacy, he is certainly privileged to maintain it.

Some fear to appear naked in front of a member of the opposite sex. Often this fear disappears as the two grow closer. Or perhaps some always feel more comfortable if they are clothed most of the time. There are no rules, except maybe this one: Most authorities believe it is not wise for parents to appear naked in front of children. Children live in a society where people do not walk around nude, and children are not given preparation for reality if their parents constantly display their nudity in front of them.

But even more important is the fact that a parent who insists on appearing naked in front of his child may be unconsciously seducing the child. Children have enough trouble coping with their strong feelings of sexuality without being further stimulated by seeing parents roam about the house stark naked. This sort of procedure may lead children to indulge in the wildest of fantasies as a way of handling their aroused emotions, and too intense a fantasy life may be a factor in creating emotional illness.

Each of us must have the freedom to live with a certain amount of privacy and it is the wise wife and husband who knows this, and is thoughtful of the other's moods. Too great a demand for closeness may destroy a marriage. It is often helpful for each to have friends of his own in addition to mutual friends.

We Are Always Alone

Those who are emotionally mature tread the middle path between loneliness and clinging closeness. In a sense we are always alone, no matter how much intimacy evolves in marriage, no matter how many children. The acceptance of this fact enables us to give more to the moments shared.

The one who shrieks, "I *won't* be alone. I married to get rid of loneliness," will find himself very much alone. No one can dispel someone else's loneliness. Any attempt to escape by placing upon one's mate the burden of easing this essential aloneness is bound to fail. This octopus clutch often strangles the very closeness the clutcher hopes to achieve.

What Shall We Talk About?

But there is one respect in which it is advisable that there be as close communion as possible. Recent research by sociologists and psychologists interested in the study of marriage shows that the husband and the wife who have the most interests in common are happier than those with different interests. Companionship, a very important ingredient of marriage, is easier for those with many of the same interests. Usually a couple have some interests in common, some different, and it is the ability to share that adds to happiness.

It is advisable to have a few mutual interests because married couples do not spend all their time in bed, fantasy of some single persons to the contrary. Lack of even one common interest may create a great gap in marriage as couples find they have nothing to talk to each other about.

The difference between a man and a woman is great enough so that not many additional differences are needed. That is why it is frequently difficult, although not impossible, for a couple, each of whom is strongly committed to a different religious faith or grew up in a very dissimilar background, to work out the problems of marriage.

There are those who refuse to become interested in anything the mate does, and then wonder why the marriage falls to pieces. Some women who are plagued by feelings of inferiority to men, rather than accepting the difference between the sexes, refuse to do anything that will further enhance what they believe to be their husband's already superior position. They are competing with him rather than complementing him.

Disinterest in a partner's achievements has various causes. It may be envy or anger or lack of real concern for the other, for if we are interested in someone we care about anything he might do, be it digging ditches or painting contemporary masterpieces. Disinterest also may be fear that the mate's success will take him away, that we will no longer be needed and thus we are threatened by any achievement on his part.

One man, who held a job as editor with a publishing company, noticed that whenever he spent a few hours on week ends working on a novel he was writing, his wife would become difficult and demanding. She felt he was taking what little time was left over from his daily work away from the children and herself in order to make himself a success. Actually, she was concerned lest he become a famous novelist, lose interest in her, and seek other, more desirable women, leaving her in the coldness of a lonely void.

The conversations of husbands and wives who are elaborately disinterested in each other's lives sound like two solo performances carried on before an unlistening audience. One man tried at great length to interest his wife in his Ph.D. dissertation on a vital political theme. While most of his friends showed intense interest, his wife could not care less. For five years he found himself unable to complete the dissertation, with serious disadvantage to his career. Finally, he realized the hostility that lay in her disinterest and was able to complete his thesis only by vowing to do it despite her. He realized, too, his dependence on her approval which had given him an alibi for not finishing the work.

Here both sides of the problem are expressed: his intense

need to involve his wife in his activities, and her inability to share even discussion of them. Some men work themselves into the ulcer-bearing, harried, high-pressured executive in an effort to win their wife's applause as they once tried to win their mother's plaudits for childhood accomplishments.

The opposite of complete disinterest, and equally as destructive, is shown by the mate who refuses to be disinterested in anything. He insists on knowing his partner's every move, every thought. One husband complained distractedly that his wife was driving him insane by constantly demanding, "What are you thinking about?"

"Not only does she follow me from room to room, peering over my shoulder at everything I read or eat, she even tries to follow me into the bathroom," he groaned. "But worst of all, I feel she is always trying to creep into my brain so she can experience every thought at the same moment I think it."

This wife had been raised in a home where her father almost completely disregarded her. Her image of man was of a preoccupied figure hiding behind book, newspaper, and cloud of cigar smoke. She was desperately attempting to make up for the exclusion she had felt as a child because of her father's withdrawal (undoubtedly she helped to cause the withdrawal by her constant curiosity) by seeking to know everything her husband was doing and thinking. She was also imitating her role with her mother to whom she had been close, who would pour out her heart to her daughter, telling her all she thought and did as the daughter listened avidly.

We cannot possibly know all that another is thinking, nor should we try. It is enough for us to know what we ourselves think. We must be content with what they wish to tell us. Why must we ask more than this? Why do we need to force them to share, rather than to accept what they are willing to give?

Too Much Together

Each one must lead his own life, even in marriage. This is an extra difficulty for those married couples who spend the days together as well as the evenings. Some husbands and wives try to work together professionally or in business, not realizing the tough situation they may be setting up for themselves.

Two talented musicians, husband and wife, went on a concert tour as duo pianists just after they were married. Before long they found themselves engaged in endless quarrels. In addition, the husband found himself increasingly attracted by other women. He realized that what he needed was separation from the constant involvement even with the wife he loved. Since most of their experiences were now mutual they had little to exchange when they talked together over supper, as contrasted with couples who went their separate ways during the day and exchanged experiences at night. Having interests in common is not the same as being together twenty-four hours a day.

There are married couples, although they are rare, who are able to work, as well as live, together. Some do it in the belief they are fighting hand in hand against a hostile world. Others have the ability, out of the richness of their own emotional life, to maintain their individuality even though working together. They are able to exchange easily their reactions, impressions, and other meaningful experiences. They do not lose a sense of identity in the joint venture to which each feels free to make his unique contribution.

One sign of emotional maturity is being able to accept someone who is different from the self. The child, like the emotionally immature person, sees everyone in the image of himself. He uses other people as a mirror in which he can narcissistically admire his own image. If they dare to differ from him, he becomes enraged, as he does when they reflect back his own inadequacies. He cannot countenance any departure, no matter how minute, from his own way of thinking and feeling and acting.

The emotionally mature person welcomes differences, accepts them as stimulating, and realizes they add spice to his life. He does not need to demand that the one he loves conform to his way of existence. He grants his mate, as well as every other human being, the dignity of difference.

6   THE PYGMALION COMPLEX

"I couldn't have picked a worse husband if I had deliberately set out to do so," wailed one wife.

"Perhaps you did," commented an intuitive friend.

The friend was saying that something in this wife knew in advance her marriage would not work but she was unable to listen to that still, small voice which so often speaks inner truth. She was too desperately driven by that part of her that sought a man who would treat her as this one did, blame her for the failure of the marriage, and criticize her every mannerism and act.

"You don't speak loudly enough in company, you cook badly, you're a lousy hostess—" From morning until night her husband's conversation was one long complaint.

At first she tried to please him, reveling in the few moments when he deigned to bestow his approval on her. She also tried to change as best she could when he would scream at her, "I can't stand you as you are! You've got to change."

Finally she realized she could never please him, that no woman in the world could, for what he demanded was impossible for any human to fulfill. It came out of his unrealistic fantasies of what a woman should be—superhuman, a goddess, the eternal "good mother" which his mother had never been, for she was a cruel, selfish, complaining woman.

If we marry expecting our partner to change, we are apt to face profound disappointment, even granted the wish of the mate to change in the desired direction. People rarely change basically, unless they have the help of a psychoanalyst, and even then they change only slowly, and perhaps some are able only to modify their personality so that they can function better.

If a mate antagonizes to the point where his partner must criticize him constantly, the partner might remember it was he who chose this once overidealized mate. The fault lies in his overidealization, not in the person he is now verbally tearing to shreds.

The characteristics we dislike in people are often their inadequate defenses against anxiety, for it is the defenses that sometimes constitute the unlovely aspects of a person. Unattractive as they are to others, the defenses serve a purpose for the one defending himself against feelings he believes dangerous. Defenses spring into being because we believe we need them in order to survive (some we really need, some we do not; they stem from our fantasies). They are a protective device, much as armor served the medieval knight, protecting but also making it more difficult to maneuver. Defenses usually will not fall except with psychological help, and anyone who attacks a defense may be hated.

It is also true that the very defenses we cannot stand in someone else are usually those within ourselves to which we are conveniently blind but which we nonetheless may secretly hate. When we condemn someone else, we are really condemning the same thing inside ourselves. The woman who berates another as "such a terrible gossip" is often the most terrible of gossips herself. The man who severely criticizes another's philandering, is either himself a Don Juan or wishes with all his heart he dared be.

Defenses do not appear out of the blue after one has married. They have long been part of the personality, most of them since childhood.

"Lord, I never realized my wife was such a nag," groaned one husband. Yet, thinking back, he recalled that during courtship she had irritated him occasionally by insisting that he should wear overshoes when it rained. But he had rationalized this as tender and appealing concern for his welfare. After a few months of marriage during which she tried to control him more and more, he felt he could not continue to live with her unless she changed. She could not, of course, because a defense as deep-rooted as nagging stems from unconscious sources which the average person is powerless to control. It is not that people *will* not change but that they *cannot* without help if the change involves what seems to them a vital part of their personality.

"I Love You as You Are"

If we realize that defenses stem from fear and not malignance, it is easier to get along with someone. One woman, whose husband would burst into anger occasionally, realized he did so when he felt insecure or fearful or unhappy. Instead of responding with rage, which she had done formerly, she now became tender to him at such times, understanding it was then he most needed love and reassurance.

One evening, after drinking more than usual at a party, he took an instant dislike to one of the guests. Instead of ridiculing him for not staying sober, or icily ignoring him, his wife asked quietly, "Would you like to go home?"

He looked at her with relief. "Would you?" he asked.

"Let's," she said, and made apologies to the hostess for leaving early.

Later that night he tried to make love to her, but he had taken in so much alcohol that he was unsuccessful. Instead of getting angry, as once she would have done, thinking this meant he did not love her, she drew him close and he soon fell asleep, not, however, before telling her how much he loved her, words he had not uttered in weeks.

Another wife, in bed with her husband, wanted him to make love to her only to have him say angrily, "There are times I just don't feel like it."

Instead of feeling hurt and rejected, she laughed softly and said, "Are there? You know that just didn't occur to me," and patted him tenderly on the shoulder.

Whereupon he turned and embraced her saying gruffly, "Yes, but tonight's not one of them."

If we can realize that most of the acts that come across to us as angry and hurtful are caused by fear, this is half the battle won, because then we do not get angry in return but understand and can be compassionate. We will not take what someone does personally, unless it is constant or devastating, but know that it stems from their fears and unresolved conflicts.

This is true acceptance of the other person as he is, and it is love if we can do this, rather than insisting he change to fit our image of the perfect human being.

"I love you just as you are"—the finest tribute in the world. It is all that many of us want to hear, some even feel it is all they need ever hear to be happy.

It is helpful if both husband and wife are able to tell each other what they admire in each other. Many find this difficult, one reason being they have heard so much empty praise and so many false compliments that they fear being considered hypocritical.

Know the True Targets

The need to change someone often springs from the childhood wish that one's parents would change. The scream, "Change! Change!" when hurled at a mate may really be hurled at one's parents. It sometimes represents an attempt to remake the marriage partner over in the image of the perfect parent—not the parent one actually had, but the parent one *wishes* he had possessed, the good parent. It is the parent idealized beyond all reality, the omnipotent omniscient parent of every infant's dream.

One woman left her husband because he continually told her what to do and how to do it. "I couldn't even brush my teeth without his instructing me in what he thought the correct way, as though I were an idiot who could not get along by myself," she explained.

Then she realized this was the very characteristic in her mother that would infuriate her to the point of speechlessness. She had selected this man because he was like her mother, the familiar, and then could not stand him because of it, demanding that he change, although never daring to ask this of her own mother.

The "in-law" conflict is one that causes much unhappiness to many couples. When it exists, there sometimes is too deep an attachment to the mother on the part of both husband and wife. Each resents in the other the failure to break free from this attachment, not seeing in himself his own dependency on his mother.

For instance, a husband who outwardly detests his wife's

mother because of her influence on his wife, may well be suppressing toward his own mother feelings of rage because she has kept him dependent.

One wife noticed that every time her father came to visit, her husband would throw a temper tantrum and hiss at her, "Get him out of the house as fast as you can." He was extremely jealous of the close relationship between his wife and her father. This was a man whose attachment to his own mother was very intimate and he would think nothing of asking her to the house to spend long week ends with them.

When there is "in-law" trouble, each must look honestly at his own feelings toward *his* parent and see if he is not projecting them upon the parent of the mate. He must recognize his own childish dependency, his fear, perhaps, of becoming angry at his mother or father, an anger which he so easily transfers toward the mate's parents.

A number of men may be unconsciously still seeking a mother, rather than a wife, and this becomes clearly evident in their relationship to their mother-in-law. It is surprising how many men have fantasies of being, or actually become, sexually involved with a mother-in-law. Those who express deep hatred may be defending themselves against expression of these sexual feelings which go back to the repressed sexual feelings they felt for their own mother, natural at a certain age but, if not dealt with, a conflict all the the rest of life. If they still suffer from guilt because of childhood sexual interest in their mother, they may be overwhelmed with guilt at all later sexual feelings. Extreme traumatic experiences in later life frequently stir up and relate to our childhood memories.

Some people may be supersensitive to remarks they construe as a demand to change but which are meant in a friendly manner. A perceptive, insightful wife several times pointed out to her husband various aspects of his behavior which she thought harmful to him, always speaking in a soft, gentle voice.

He turned to her one day and said angrily, "You claim you love me so much and yet why do you find things wrong with me?"

She replied thoughtfully, "I love you as you are. But I also see in you such a wonderful potential that if I can help you in any small way to achieve it, not for myself but for you, I feel I should try."

She was expressing the natural wish that each of us holds for our loved ones that they live up to their fullest capacity. It is a sad fact that most of us go through life never reaching our full potential either in our work or our ability to love. Knowing this, the art of living with someone is to steer the delicate course between demanding they change and being indifferent to their capabilities.

The Tyranny of Control

Some enter marriage with the idea of trying to change their mate as the central aim of the marriage, acknowledged or unacknowledged. One intelligent career woman married a man seven years younger than she. He was a comparatively unsuccessful musician and she decided that what he needed was her strong hand to make him a success. He, on the other hand, was determined to give up his musical career and become a college instructor in history which he had long wished to do.

She spent a stormy two years of marriage attempting to discourage him from continuing with his studies in history, urging him to return to his violin. He fought her as best he could but finally gave up the struggle to teach, left graduate school, and became once again an unsuccessful, musician sawing away as a gypsy violinist in a small restaurant. It was as though he were saying to her, "Okay. If you want me to be a musician, I'll be one, but a failure."

She realized, after the marriage ended in disaster, that what she had craved was not a fully formed man but one she could fashion to her taste. A number of women seem to possess this need. It grows partially out of their maternal wish to create a child and partially out of a neurotic wish to control another human being's destiny as they felt controlled by their parents. The woman who feels free herself has less need to control anyone else, for she realizes how damaging this may be to the relationship.

Men attempt such control, too. One successful attorney while traveling through the South met and fell in love with a singer he heard in a rather inelegant night club. After a whirlwind courtship of two weeks, he married her and brought her back to the sophisticated circles in which he moved in New York's café society. He spent the next three years trying to make her into a successful singer. He almost bankrupted himself hiring the best teachers and vocal coaches, paying for special musical arrangements, and buying her the most exclusive of gowns, all apparently to no avail.

At first she was so overwhelmed by his interest, his position, and his friends that she passively went along trying to do what he so anxiously wished. But then she grew desperate because of her inability to live up to the ambitions he outlined for her. Finally, when she felt she could stand it no longer and was ready to leave him because it seemed to her that he would not be able to face the failure of his plans for her, she had the courage to say, "Look. I don't want any of this. I married you because I wanted to be your wife, to have your children, and to make a home for us."

Fortunately, he understood, and told her he loved her

whether or not she was a success. Today, with one child born and a second on the way, it seems as if he has given up his wish to play Pygmalion to her reluctant Galatea.

If he had not been able to relinquish his desire to create a wife in the image of his fantasy of her, their marriage would have been doomed. For whether or not she had the talent requisite for success in so highly competitive a field as night-club singing, his insistence on her changing aroused within her great unspoken resentment. She felt as if he were saying to her, "You are not good enough the way you are. I must make you over into somebody more worthwhile."

In addition to the resentment over being manipulated, she felt a strong resistance to any change, since, like most of us, she wanted to be loved just as she was and not for her acomplishments, not even for her beauty. To have become a successful singer would have meant to her that she was loved not for herself alone but for what she had achieved.

You Can't "Make" Someone Else Happy or Successful

In many marriages the demand is not this extreme but it is nevertheless present as a constant undercurrent of discontent and, like all undercurrents, a perpetual threat. There are wives determined to make their husbands a success. Many comic strips, movies, and television serials help to perpetuate the myth that American men are blithering idiots who have to be led carefully by the hand by their practical, sane, right-thinking wives in order to succeed in any endeavor. Some women act out this mythical role indulging their unconscious wishes for mastery over the man by striving with might and main to manipulate him so he will be a success. They identify with him far too closely for their own good or his and usually end up, as Craig's wife did, in the play of that name, alone and abandoned.

It is difficult for anyone to "make" somebody else into a success any more than they can really "make" someone else happy. If one is happy, it is usually a result of his own doings, just as is his unhappiness. It is easy to blame someone else for our failure, or give him credit for our victory, but it is rarely the whole truth. It is a psychic fact that no one can "do" anything to us without some aid from ourselves. We are often unwitting accomplices to our own destruction. We may wish not to believe this, but if we insist on refusing to be responsible for our unhappiness, we also deny to ourselves the strength to do anything about achieving happiness.

One woman married a talented young poet and decided to "make" him into an advertising copy writer so he would be able to earn money, for poets are notoriously poverty-stricken. Being a person of considerable determination and charm, she sought and found a position for him in an advertising agency. He found himself so appalled and anxiety-stricken at the thought of working on Madison Avenue, which he had satirized in some of his poetry, that she went to the office with him every morning and waited around to lunch with him in order to give him the courage to continue with the job.

She talked of this at cocktail parties within full hearing of her husband who never gave any surface indication of being upset but would join in singing her praises over how helpful she had been to his career. Since he was highly skilled in the use of words, eventually he became a proficient advertising copy writer. She then obtained an even better position for him in a firm in which one of her relatives held a financial interest.

Strangely enough, this marriage has lasted for twenty years and seems reasonably successful, but such a marriage requires the almost perfect and miraculous mesh of two contradictory neurotic characters. He is an essentially passive man, pleased to have the direction of a strong, feminine mind. She has a great need to control all her relationships and he was the first man she found willing to permit her this measure of control. In a previous relationship with a man to whom she was very much attracted, she had been unable to effect any permanent tie because he refused to permit her to take over the guidance and direction of his life.

Usually the attempt to change someone ends in tragedy. One earthy, levelheaded young architect married an over-sensitive young lady who was very vulnerable to every nuance of feeling. From the first day he met her, she strove constantly to make him more "sensitive," more tender, more responsive to her feelings.

Incidentally, there is a difference between sensitivity and perception. To be perceptive entails knowing reality and is based on the awareness and acceptance of the self. Sensitivity, on the other hand, often arises from defending the self against attack, and is comprised of projection, narcissism, and even paranoia-like reactions. It focuses on the self, not reality.

The wife mentioned above lacked perceptiveness as she tried to make over her husband in her own image. At first he tried dutifully to please her, attempting to develop the sensitivity she valued so highly. However, as the unremitting struggle to produce this sensitivity in him became more difficult, he grew bored, then enraged with what he felt was an attempt to make him into something he was not and could not be.

Putting his foot down, he told her in no uncertain terms to stop trying to change him. But she was unable to halt her compulsive drive to remake him, believing that he was afraid to realize himself as the full, sensitive human he could become. The conflict grew too intense for them to stay married.

This woman's mother had been an insensitive, critical, depriving woman and her father, preoccupied with financial worries, rarely had time to pay attention to his daughter. When she married, she tried to create a husband who would make up for all of her past deprivations, one who would be a combination of the loving mother, constantly aware of her infant's needs, and the strong, protective father who had time, energy, and the interest to help his child develop fully. While her need was understandable, it was unrealistic, since no adult can make up for the care and love one missed in infancy. Too, we must remember that the child, in his demand for love and attention, is insatiable, and one of the signs of maturity is the ability to give up insatiability.

There Is No Magic

Many, in their marriage, are searching for the perfect parent who will do for them as once was done by their mother. The infant in the crib is cold and wet and, magically, soft hands caress him and make him dry and warm. He is hungry and, magically, a full breast or bottle appears to ease his hunger.

All this is done without his even voicing a request. Although this magic ends for the most part when we leave the crib, to some this was such a pleasurable time of life that they try to duplicate it forever after, screaming for the magic to reappear, especially if later periods prove so dangerous that they fear to move out of their former dependence to try to stand alone.

The pampered child is often a frightened child. Sometimes

he is even less prepared to deal with life than the neglected child who is accustomed to frustration. The pampered child may be an overindulged child but he pays a terrific psychic price for this indulgence just as the neglected child pays for his lack of any pampering which he then yearns for desperately.

Indulgence is not always the same as love—it is often the easy way out for the parent who thinks he is winning the affection of the child by granting his every wish, little realizing how difficult he is making it for the child in later life when he cannot possibly have his every wish. He will find it very difficult to make friends, let alone lasting relationships, unless he can accept frustrations. It is a sad sight to see grown men or women throwing temper tantrums, as though they were still children, when they cannot be granted the smallest of their wishes.

It is everybody's birthright to feel beloved. Children are born with the right to be loved, but when you are an adult you sometimes have to earn love by being lovable. Emotionally immature adults feel, "I want to be the same as I was when I was little and my mother loved me just as I was, and why can't my mate?" A child is entitled to many actions unbefitting an adult. It is difficult, if not impossible, for most of us to love an adult who insists on acting like a child or an adolescent. He may be amusing or diverting for an evening but he is no one with whom most of us would wish to spend our entire lives.

Demands Do Not Help

In a successful marriage some may slowly change, but it is a change that occurs not in response to a demand but comes out of the stimulation of living together. It is a change best accomplished by example, one to the other, rather than preaching. Deeds, not words, achieve it.

A husband who tends to be overinvolved with his business will more likely pay greater attention to the needs of his wife if she gives him an example through her own behavior, being more thoughtful of him, rather than if she demands that he consider her needs. Her demand may make it impossible for him to change even if he were to wish to do so consciously, since it is human to feel that we deprive ourselves of our own individuality if we do something because someone else demands it, not because it comes from our own heart. The husband may even conform, but if he does so unwillingly the act will be meaningless; and it may lay the groundwork for increasing resentment.

One man was married to a woman who lived in constant alarm caused by many petty fears. She worried needlessly about such possible misfortunes as lacking enough money to pay bills, or fear of burglars breaking into the house, or being struck down by sudden illness. Rather than insisting she stop this foolishness, as some husbands would have done, he understood that it masked deeper fears which he was not qualified to interpret, and so he said nothing to her. Through his own casualness and refusal to worry, he demonstrated that her fears were unreal. After awhile she was able to profit by his example and slowly gave up much of her useless worrying.

This husband made no demand on his wife to change. To live in comfort with someone, we must be careful of the demands we make. They are most likely to be demands on ourselves which we feel unable to fulfill. If we must make demands of someone else, we must look first at what it is we are demanding and then ask ourselves why we make the demand.

The very act of marriage implies that each partner is willing to undertake a certain amount of responsibility. But it is not the demands inherent in this responsibility that create trouble in marriage. It is, rather, the demands that arise out of excessive personal needs that have little to do with the demands that come out of the marriage.

When each one is able to handle his own inner conflicts and not demand that the other make life happy for him by metamorphosis into the imagined perfect parent, this is movement in the direction of marital maturity.

"You're driving me crazy!"

This is one of the most frequent reproaches that husbands and wives address to each other, either out loud or in their minds, as they feel the other assaults them with unreason.

One example of the kind of behavior that makes a husband or wife feel the other is intent on forcing him out of his wits was shown by a wife whose husband was building his own boat during week ends at a yard near their home. As he set out one Sunday morning for the boat yard, she asked bitterly, "Are you going to work on that boat again today?"

"I thought I would," he said, uncertainty in his voice. "Was there anything you wanted me to do?"

"No," she said, her voice a mixture of disappointment and tears.

"If there is, I'll stay home," he offered unhappily.

"It's just that the children don't see you very often," she said, adding defiantly, "Nor do I."

"Come on down and help me," he said impulsively. "You can paint."

She shuddered. "It's too hot to work in the sun."

He sighed. "I'll give up the damned boat. It isn't worth it."

"You'd be very unhappy. I know how much it means to you," she said in a martyred tone.

The husband did not know what to do. He felt he had no way out, that no matter how he resolved the conflict, both she and he would be unhappy about the decision. If he went on his way, he would feel guilty and she would sulk, and if he stayed home, she would feel guilty and he would resent her for forcing him to give up his hobby.

Between husband and wife, as between parent and child, this kind of situation may be duplicated endlessly as one makes the other feel so hopelessly confused that there seems no escape except madness, a route sometimes taken by those who give up completely.

Men and women who grew up in a family where they frequently experienced this treatment at the hands of parents are particularly sensitive to such an impasse for some parents use such subtle pressure as a means of control.

One young woman was the only daughter of a widowed mother who had lost her husband when the girl was three years old. The mother worked hard as secretary in a large insurance firm in order to support her daughter and send her through college. No sacrifice was too great for the mother to make in her daughter's behalf, as she often pointed out to her daughter.

The mother was excessively controlling of her daughter's behavior. She would demand that the daughter dress in fashions she chose, go out with only certain men, behave toward them in ways that she outlined, and she supervised equally assiduously her daughter's choice of women friends. But never was this control exercised with anger or dictation. It was always rather, "Joan, I just want the best for you. I'm

trying as hard as I can to make you happy. You are all I have
in life."

While the daughter dimly perceived her mother was not
permitting her to become an individual by allowing her to
make her own mistakes, she dared not be angry at a mother
so self-sacrificing, so thoughtful of her, and thus found it
impossible to break loose from the silken web of what was
really a ruthless, though subtly expressed, tyranny. Her
mother's very kindness made the control all the more difficult
to bear. If her mother had been brutally dominating, Joan
might have been able to express her differences.

Eventually, when she felt herself on the verge of losing her
mind, the daughter broke with a vengeance from her mother's
direct domination. She moved to a distant city where, for
several years, she staged a riotous rebellion, seeking the company of men and women of whom no mother could possibly
approve. Then she got married, thinking this would solve
her problems. But after marriage she would alternate between short, fitful periods of intense activity and long periods
of inert withdrawal during which life seemed too agonizing
for her and she would lie in bed for hours, seething with a
vague, helpless rage.

When her husband tried to rouse her from one of these
lethargic states saying, "I am only trying to do what's best
for you," she hurled herself at him with tigerlike ferocity,
threw dishes, overturned a bookcase, and smashed phono-
graph records in her fury at hearing words that reminded
her of her hated enslavement to her mother.

The Bind That Destroys

Although not to the extreme just described, this type of
tenuous tyranny is so common that a special term has been de-

vised for it—the double bind. It was thus named by four social scientists, Gregory Bateson, Don D. Jackson, Jay Haley, and John Weakland. They first described it in an article titled "Toward a Theory of Schizophrenia," which appeared in the October 1956, issue of *Behavioral Science,* a quarterly journal which is the official publication of Mental Health Research of the University of Michigan.

The authors described the double bind as a situation in which, no matter what a person does, "he can't win." He feels helpless, fearful, exasperated, and raging. He senses he is being indicted for a crime he does not understand and did not commit, and in turn he fears the one who makes him suffer so.

The double bind is based on the inability of two people to communicate their feelings to each other, which means that each is not facing his true feelings. It starts in childhood, between mother and child. If extreme at this early age, it may cause schizophrenia, the four researchers declare.

"We must expect pathology to occur in people when there is a breach in the communication between mother and child," they state. "We shall argue that this pathology at its extreme will have symptoms whose formal characteristics would lead the pathology to be classified as schizophrenia."

The extreme situation consists not of one traumatic experience but experiences that are repeated over and over in the life of a child. As the child becomes the adult, he expects to be caught in the double bind in all his relationships, for his relationship with his mother is the model for the rest of life. He unconsciously seeks out the double bind, provoking it in those to whom he tries to become close, choosing a mate who has a propensity to inflict the double bind upon him.

The double bind in childhood operates thus. A child approaches his mother and tries to kiss and hug her to show his affection. She receives his advances with coldness, perhaps pushing him away, perhaps saying, "Not now," or "Don't be silly," perhaps saying nothing but giving him a condemning look or a shrug of the shoulders, which tells him she does not approve of his show of emotion. Whereupon the child feels ashamed, guilty, and punished, and withdraws.

Then, expressing the other half of the bind, the mother, out of her own guilt, seeks to re-establish the original situation where the child will again embrace her. She may tease him or flirt with him or accuse him of not loving her, until he responds anew with affection. Again frightened, she rejects his love as she did before. At this point, the baffled child knows not which way to turn. He is being seduced and rejected, seduced and rejected, and these swings between seduction and rejection, if they are violent, are what causes psychosis, according to the authors.

They illustrate the extreme double bind with the example of a visit between a young man, a patient in a mental hospital, and his mother. He had just recovered from a severe psychotic state and, glad to see her, impulsively threw his arms around her.

She stiffened and withdrew. He took his arms away, lowered his head in guilt, as if expecting punishment.

She then asked, "Don't you love me any more?"

He blushed and was silent. She went on, "Dear, you must not be afraid of your feelings."

After she left, he attacked an attendant and had to be given hydrotherapy to calm him down.

Damned Whatever One Does

In the double-bind situation, there is no consistency in the child's emotional life, for he never knows what to expect. He cannot use his reason, as yet undeveloped, to realize that his mother has her own fears and guilts, to realize, too, that perhaps her rejection of him may be healthier than if she gave vent to her impulses and fully encouraged the expression of his urges with the end result, years later, either of actual sexual intimacy between parent and child, or so deep a sexual attachment that the child, as an adult, can never break free.

Although the authors do not state this, the incest taboo is probably one of the causes of the double bind, the fear of the mother of her own sexual feelings for the child. Another cause is the conflict between love and hate that lies in all of us, unresolved in those who fear to express feelings of love and hate because both emotions somehow have become too dangerous to them. When one has difficulty exploring emotions, all communication becomes difficult.

The child who is victim of the double bind (and we all are, to some extent) is caught in a situation where, if he responds to his mother's affection, her anxiety will be aroused and she will punish him, thus confusing him about the nature of his own feelings, in order to defend herself from closeness with him. But if he makes no overtures of affection, she feels this means she is not a loving mother, and this also will arouse her anxiety, and she will either punish him by withdrawing or make overtures toward him, insisting he demonstrate once again that he loves her. If he then responds and shows affection, she will not only feel once again endangered, but may also resent the fact that she had to force him to respond this time.

The child feels he will be punished for a show of love, punished also if he does not show it. As the authors state, "the impossible dilemma" for the child becomes, "If I am to keep my tie to my mother I must not show her that I love her, but if I do not show her that I love her, then I will lose her."

Losing a parent to a child means his psychological death, for he cannot reason or fend for himself in an adult world; he needs his mother to survive.

The double bind is re-enacted in an adult relationship when someone encourages his mate to show affection, then, out of fear of his own sexual feelings, withdraws, whereupon the mate feels hurt and punished. Then the rejecting one makes overtures and, when the mate responds, again there is the retreat and refusal to show affection, plus anger over being forced to encourage the overtures.

The authors also mention the feeling of abandonment on the part of the child that results from the expression of extreme helplessness by the parent. When a parent is unable to face his own feelings, how can a child, far more uncontrollable and versed not at all in logic and thoughtfulness, hope to face his feelings?

Too, when we feel that someone does not want us, in defense against our hurt we may believe or tell ourselves that we do not want him. A child who feels thus about his mother is swept by desolation, for he has no one else to whom he can turn.

The double bind can be effectively masked under the guise of love and solicitude or it may be expressed in other ways. One man came home to find his wife in tears. She explained that their twelve-year-old son had stolen two bottles of wine from the liquor cabinet. Helplessly she turned to her husband and pleaded, "You've got to do something about it."

He called the boy into his study and questioned him. He discovered his son had stolen the wine at the instigation of an older boy in the neighborhood with whom his son was anxious to be friendly and had given the bottles to the older boy who had hidden them in anticipation of a get-together the next night, when he and several others would experiment to find out what it felt like to be drunk.

At first the father wanted to march over to the older boy's house, inform his parents of the theft, and get back the wine. But when the son pleaded with him not to do so, for it would make him an outcast with his friends, the father agreed to let the boy himself manage the return of the pilfered bottles.

As the son left the house on his mission, the wife, who had overheard the entire conversation, walked up to her husband and said accusingly, "Why are you trying to humiliate your son? For two bottles of wine you want to make him the laughingstock of all his friends?"

The husband felt he had handled the matter quite well before his wife's attack. When now she criticized him for doing exactly what she had asked him to do, he became enraged. They plunged into a heated fight during which he had to restrain himself from attacking her physically. He felt that she was deliberately driving him crazy, first asking him to take action and then condemning him for what he did. His rage was, in part, created by her confusion but also, in large part, touched off by the resemblance it bore to his mother's behavior when she would urge him as a boy to stay home and study so he would do well at school and then would want to know why he was not out playing with the other boys when he curled up with a book.

Thus also acted a mother who asked her adolescent son, "Why are you home all the time? Why don't you go out more?" and then, when he started to have dates every Saturday night, complained, "You're never home."

Killing with Kindness

It is this attitude which often causes the Alphonse and Gaston routine between couples as each one urges the other to make the decision as to where to go for an evening's entertainment or what make of car to buy or in which apartment or house to live. Each prefers the other to arrive at the decision in order to gain approval, to avoid being criticized for the wrong choice, and sometimes to have the doubtful pleasure of being the one to criticize.

Although this deferring is an attempt to avoid criticism, of course it does not, because the deferrer is then castigated as a coward, too weak to make decisions. Here the attempt to evade criticism by refusing to accept responsibility fails because then the criticism is directed at the very attempt to escape it.

Sometimes the double bind is never put into words. One man carefully refrained from ever asking his wife for any special dishes at dinner. Each time she asked what he would prefer to eat that night, he would reply, "Anything you like, dear." Although he was often dissatisfied with what she served, he never expressed this openly but she would know how he felt by his lack of enthusiasm over the meal.

In this way, as he kept his wife constantly striving to guess what he wanted, she could not accuse him of making demands. She felt confused, uncertain, because on the surface he seemed such a compliant husband, always saying, "Whatever you like, dear," yet she felt his unspoken demands were gigantic for he really was asking that she know what he wanted without his having to take the responsibility of stating the request. His demands were so great, he dared not make even one.

Along with the fear of making any demand went his feeling that his wife was unjust, the world was unjust, and he could never really get what he wanted anyhow. He was correct, since what he wanted was impossible for anyone to give him, a continual reading of his mind and the granting of his every wish.

Similarly, in business he could never ask his associates for what he felt his due but would nurse deep unspoken resentment because he believed he was treated unfairly. He was unable to make his requests explicit, yet became angry when his unspoken requests were not granted, as if others should be able to know what he wanted.

I Love You—I Hate You

Probably ever since Adam and Eve, a subtle exchange of feeling between two lovers has existed, the bind of both love and hate, of giving and withdrawing at alternate moments (possibly even existing in the years before man could speak but lived on earth in silence). If the love and hate swings are too extreme, the effect is one of bewilderment, perhaps even paralysis, on the part of those caught in it.

This is shown clearly in a very effective film, part of the extensive study of the double bind carried out by Gregory Bateson and his colleagues. The movie shows a mother seated on a couch talking to a visitor as her child walks over and tries to get her attention. She turns toward him with a maternal smile, answers his question, then, when he does not go away but stands looking at her wistfully, twitches her foot impatiently in his direction as though to kick him, and twists her body away from him in anger, as though to tell him to drop dead. Her words may be loving but she is getting across to him in these few moments, with her body, her facial expression, her gestures, and tone of voice, that she also is angry and irritated. The child becomes confused as to what she really feels—is it the spoken language of her tongue or the unspoken language of her body?

This is the essence of the double bind—I want you near me; I don't want you near me. It is displayed by the mother who hugs her child furiously one minute, then slaps him the next, and by the wife who snaps at her husband in fury but all the while wants him to make love to her.

The mother with her child and the wife with her boat-building husband engaged in the double bind as a form of control without making the control explicit. There may lie in this hidden control quite an element of hatred. But the mother could not admit to herself that, at moments, she hated the child, just as the wife could not admit she felt some hatred for her husband for not understanding her wish.

The danger in the double bind is that you can never face the enemy. You cannot challenge the attacker, for the latter will not openly confess his hatred and unspoken demands, so you feel perpetually crucified.

If you are the one responsible for initiating the double bind, the danger is that you are deceiving yourself about what you feel and, at the same time, destroying the love the other person holds for you, because your actions are bound to arouse hostility in him.

A parent who may feel guilty because of a moment's ardent embrace of a child, is apt to fling the child away from him immediately after the caress because of his fear of displaying such a hungry love. The wife mentioned above actually wanted her husband at home instead of at the boat yard, hoping he would make love to her, hating him for not having done so the night before when they returned from a party, but she could not admit this to him.

When the husband said he would give up the boat, she could not allow him to do so because of her guilt over the unspoken request she knew she had made. Also, she realized from his tone that he did not really want to stay home, that he resented her trying to dictate to him what he should do on his day off.

It helps to realize that when there are intense feelings of anger, for instance, toward one's children, these feelings may hold something of the sexual. Recognizing this, the mature person accepts these feelings and controls them without needing to act them out or use hostility as a way of denying them. Fathers who angrily denounce a daughter's fancied immorality are often denying their own attraction to the daughter and displaying their fear that she will prefer another man to them. Mothers may also do this with sons as they tear down all young women the sons bring home as possible wives.

If married couples are able to talk over with each other how they really feel, this is one way of dealing with the double bind. If one thinks the other has driven him into an intolerable situation, he should say so quietly. He also should look within himself to find out why he feels a victim.

The double bind draws much of its malignancy from not being verbalized. To make it explicit deprives it of a large part of its capacity to maim the marriage. When the husband, whose wife complained about the boat yet refused to let him give it up, was able to explain to her how she made him feel, she then confessed to him what her unspoken wish had been, apologizing for putting her demands above any consideration of his pleasure. He understood, sympathized, and said he had been unfeeling and selfish the night before not to have sensed her wish for sexual intimacy. They laughed together, and from then on she joined him occasionally to help paint the boat. He, on the other hand, was less driven to devote every spare minute of his time to the boat. Because they were able to express their feelings about what had happened, not angrily but honestly and thoughtfully, they moved toward each other instead of apart.

If the chasm is too wide, the double bind too strong, then an intense effort may be needed to understand and destroy it. The double bind arises, as do many of our defenses, out of insecurity and fear, and sometimes these must be faced first before one can break free of its tentacles.

8 THE PLEASURE IN PAIN

To hear some wives and husbands describe their life together you would think their chief purpose in getting married was to collect a host of atrocities committed upon each one by the other "loving" partner.

One woman is so well known for this proclivity that if she does not telephone around that day to tell of the latest vicious act of her husband, her friends will say, "Fran must be getting along with Ed for a change." They know when she has some indignity to relate, she is on the telephone bright and early to report to all and sundry the latest crime committed by her husband who, according to her, puts Jack the Ripper in a class with Pollyanna.

Yet for ten years she has stayed married to a man she describes as "a beast in human form." She also speaks of her mother as "an old shrew" and her father as "a miserable tyrant." Such a woman usually does not confine her search for atrocious treatment to her mate, but will see all her relationships in similar light—it is because she has felt this way about her parents as she grew up that she chooses a man who also will make her feel mistreated.

Some seem to go through life seeking ways to suffer. They will not, cannot, give up suffering even though they complain about it endlessly. It is as though they get a kick out of their suffering. Actually, the suffering serves many psychic purposes for them.

One young woman received a call from a friend of hers, an older woman, who with her two children had just come to the city from Florida and had no place to live. The young woman invited her friend and the children to stay at her home temporarily. The older woman, in turn, offered to share the rent.

After the guests had lived with her two weeks, the younger woman began to complain to friends of the dreadful things they were doing to make her life miserable. The children were noisy and never let her sleep, morning or evening. The mother was sloppy, turning her treasured apartment into a veritable pigsty. They ate her food and the mother also drank up her liquor, never paying her share of expenses, not even the promised rent.

The young woman found it uncomfortable to go home and spent as much time as she could visiting friends and regaling them with stories of her suffering. Some of these friends, trying to help, suggested she order the older woman and her children to leave immediately and find other quarters. She refused to do this, saying she did not want to throw the children out into the street.

Meanwhile she basked in the sympathy of understanding friends who told her how magnanimous she was and seemed deeply upset by her suffering. One day one of them asked whether she had told a mutual acquaintance about the pain she was enduring, in that she could not call her home her own.

The young woman without thinking replied, "Oh, no! I'd never tell *her*. She wouldn't care. It wouldn't bother her a bit."

In these artless phrases she revealed one of the true reasons for her self-imposed rack of pain. Her suffering was a subtle way of obtaining comfort from the world and of expressing her hostility, of saying, "Look how life makes me suffer. I want everyone to suffer in return for what is happening to me." Since the mutual acquaintance, a heartless woman, would not go along with her suffering, it was pointless to pour tales of trials and tribulations into her stony ears.

It is not surprising that this same young woman who sheltered the unwelcome guests had previously been married to a man who she felt also made life torture for her. She constantly complained to all who would listen of the cruel sexual demands her husband made upon her, declaring that he was, for all his charming veneer, a coarse animal, interested only in her body.

In addition, he demanded that she keep house and prepare interesting meals regularly although she wanted a career as a singer. She felt his demands that she perform all the household tasks would make it impossible for her to devote enough time to study her singing. In struggling against his requests, she tried to anger him, uttering venomous remarks about his bestiality, his lack of feeling, and his inability to understand anything but gross appetites. When he did not respond with anger, as she expected he would, she then accused him of being a door mat who would permit any woman to walk all over him.

He accepted her attacks with remarkable equanimity, insisting only that she have a child. He apparently thought that if she had a baby she would give up her ambitions for a musical career and settle down and become the wife and mother he visualized. She refused, and when he became even more insistent, she temporized, promising to have a child the following year. When that year ended, she said she would have one the next year. Then he lost patience and gave her an ultimatum. Either she would have a child or he would divorce her. She refused, believing this the utmost cruelty, and he went through with the divorce.

Her complaints about his brutal behavior were loud and long. They also alternated with complaints about herself. Her conversation was at least consistent in that it contained complaints either about somebody else or her own miserable life.

After her divorce she became involved with a number of men, all of whom turned out to be worthless in some way and all of whom served to augment the list of her complaints. Her suffering throughout this period, while highly vocal, was nevertheless genuine. She frequently suffered real humiliation and pain at the hands of these men, even though the difficulties sometimes seemed contradictory. For example, of the first man with whom she became involved after her divorce, her great complaint was that he seemed to have no sexual need of her at all, unlike her husband who had made too many physical demands. Both men were equally cruel in her mind.

Pain Serves Many Psychic Purposes

Why do some women act like this? Why must they endure pain in the pursuit of pleasure, why should anyone deliberately court pain, physical or psychological? The word for this is "masochism" as opposed to "sadism" which is the inflicting of pain.

In the case of the young woman above, several reasons are clearly apparent. Afraid to say no to the older woman, she took on the suffering involved and then was able to attack the "guests who came to dinner" because they made her suffer. She did not realize she had asked for the suffering which a simple "no" would have avoided. Also she was then able to indulge in a veiled attack upon friends as she inflicted her misery on them—as she herself pointed out, what was the use of complaining to a friend who would not suffer for her? Complaint constitutes an oblique way of making an assault on someone, the one who must listen.

She was trying, too, to show her moral superiority, for, by getting involved in situations where others caused her pain, she thought she was proving that she was a superior person whom the rest of the world abused, the helpless victim of the cruelty of others. In this way she could deny her own responsibility for courting pain and her own inner hostility. What she might have wished to do to others was done unto her. In denouncing it in others, she was, at the same time, denouncing her own impulses to inflict pain.

Knowing something of her early life helps to make the causes of her behavior more understandable. Her mother was an irascible, angry woman who complained constantly about her husband's scandalous behavior with other women, some of it imagined, some of it real. She accused her daughter of failing to appreciate the sacrifices she made to live with this philanderer in order to keep the home together through the wretched years. She called upon the daughter to join her in denouncing the father.

The daughter was caught in a conflict between her natural affection for her father, which she tried to keep secret from her mother who would have turned upon her in fury for daring to favor such a scoundrel, and her wish to earn her mother's love by joining her in attacks on the father, for no daughter can afford a mother's hatred. Life in its early stages is too precarious without a mother's love.

As she grew up, by choosing men who would abuse her, she was faithful to the memory of her mother since she showed that she, too, recognized the brutality of all men and there-fore, of her father. Too, like many who dare not defy a tyrant but instead become tyrants and, through identification with the tyrant can show defiance toward others, she took on her mother's tyrannical attitude of assailing men as monsters.

She was also imitating what her mother had done, as daughters are likely to do, since the mother is their first and most important image of femininity. Thus she was driven into behaving like the mother whose behavior she herself found completely reprehensible. She became like her mother before her, a martyr, using the martyrdom in the service of tyranny.

The Menace of the Martyr

The martyr wife, or the martyr mother, is one of the most unhappy of all human beings with whom to be involved. Almost every contact with the other members of her family provokes her to feats of martyrdom which make Joan of Arc pale into obscurity. Even acts of nature are looked upon as a special source of pain.

One woman, whose family had planned a picnic on a day that turned out gray and drizzling, looked up at the skies and said with a bravely concealed tear in her voice, "I wanted just one day of pleasure! And I couldn't even have that," as though the rain was deliberately pouring down only to in-flict further suffering on her. She had spent the day before complaining in advance of all the hardships she would be forced to endure on the picnic.

With her continued martyrdom she managed to dominate her entire family much more effectively than any iron-fisted dictator because no decent human being would oppose her and thus add one iota to the mighty heap of pain she was al-

ready displaying to the world. The effectiveness of the
martyr's method of control arises from the difficulty of fighting it openly, unlike naked domination against which rebellion is easier.

While the martyr wife is so well known as to be almost a
stereotype, there are husbands, too, who attempt to dominate
through suffering of a different kind. One husband succeeds
in cowing his entire family by coming home night after night
worn and haggard from the day's work. He forces his wife
and children to tiptoe around the house and wait on him
hand and foot so he can maintain his slender hold on a life
which seems ebbing away because of the fierce demands he
supposedly makes upon himself to support the family.

One of the most serious problems that the martyr provokes
is the stifled rage that almost inevitably arises in the people
with whom he lives. A home with a good working martyr in
it is a home in which cheer and joy seem blasphemous, for
how could anyone have the temerity to be happy when someone is suffering so acutely?

One young woman, considered cheerful and friendly in her
social and business contacts, felt glum and depressed each
time she came home. She started to realize this was caused,
in part, by her mother's attitude of bravely holding up under
intense suffering. Each time she asked her mother how she
felt, there would be a long sigh and then the grim-lipped
statement, "Don't worry about me, dear," then another sigh,
and, "You have your own life to live. I'm all right."

Usually the daughter responded to this by questioning her
mother and trying to find out specifically what was wrong.
But the more she questioned, the deeper and more intense the
sighs and the more evasive the answers, always delivered with
a thin, deliberately transparent façade of good cheer.

Finally, as the daughter began to understand her mother's

martyrdom, she would come home as bright and cheerful as if she were with her friends. She would ask her mother how she felt and when her mother responded with the usual sighs and, "I'll be all right," the daughter took these words at their face value and said heartily, "That's great! I'm glad to hear it." She had made up her mind that she would no longer absorb, as though by osmosis, her mother's moody air of long-suffering.

Strangely enough, or perhaps not so strangely after all, as the daughter used this response more and more consistently, the mother seemed less depressed in her daughter's presence and saved her sighs and quiet agony for more vulnerable members of the family.

It is difficult for the martyr to understand his own behavior, but the family can often be helpful by disregarding the martyrdom rather than rewarding it with increased attention and concern. This is not heartless but actually the only kind of action that helps martyrs, who will not help themselves, to divest themselves temporarily of their raiments of mourning. Sackcloth and ashes look incongruous in gay company, if the company has the courage to be gay around a martyr.

The constant complainer is often one who feels hopeless of obtaining love other than through a display of suffering. Frequently he grew up with parents who were complainers and who paid him the most attention when he was sick, so he feels that the way to get people concerned is through illness and suffering. To break this pathetic cycle, the families of martyrs have to make a determined effort to show them there are far more effective ways to get love than through suffering. Suffering, unfortunately for those who rely on it as a means of getting attention, makes one quite unlovable.

One reason the masochist is so successful in dominating

those around him is that he manages to touch off some of the guilt that lies latent in all of us. Each of us has held enough death wishes for others so that we suffer some guilt because of them. The martyr's suffering is directed at making us feel that somehow we played an important part in causing it.

Some Arrange for Suffering

There are two kinds of masochistic suffering. One is displayed by those who look upon the normal vicissitudes of life as a horrific threat to their existence, which must be complained about continually. The other kind of masochism is shown by those who go to great lengths to arrange their lives so that real suffering takes place. Some combine both types in their search for the ultimate in misery.

The woman who chooses an alcoholic husband suffers in earnest, but it must be remembered that she made her choice with open eyes out of her need to endure the suffering such a marriage entails. The man who picks a shrewish wife makes a choice that enables him to undergo the pleasure of suffering. If a masochist manages to separate himself from a mate who inflicts suffering on him, usually he promptly rushes into another alliance which proves equally pain-provoking. It is evident that he unconsciously needs to suffer, for no one, unless he is severely emotionally ill, takes on suffering deliberately.

Some women need a certain display of cruelty in order to become sexually aroused. This varies from a wish for the man to be tough and hard but within the normal range of masculinity, to whippings and lashings as a prerequisite for sexual intimacy.

The popularity of many a present-day male movie star is based on the cruelty hinted at by his demeanor and behavior on the screen. One young actor leaped into stardom as a result of his first prominent role which featured him in a rape scene. Ever since then, most of the movies in which he has appeared include at least one scene in which he savagely rips the clothes off some terrified maiden with the camera panning away just before the final moment of frenzy.

Gone are the gentle, romantic, hand-kissing stars of former years, the Valentinos and Ramon Navarros, whose amorous techniques are now considered comical when glimpsed on television. In their place reign actors who, in some cases, were literally truck drivers before they rose to celluloid immortality. In all fairness, it must be said that many of those who earn their living driving trucks are among the most considerate of men. Somehow the truck driver has become a symbol of the brutal, forceful male, possibly because the powerful truck he drives unconsciously symbolizes potency so great as to be painful.

Our popular songs, too, often harp on the theme of brutality and sadism. It is difficult to think of many recent hits in which a woman speaks of her "gentle" lover. Usually the words refer to "heartless," "cruel" lovers or recite the sorrows of a woman deserted (that is, if the words make any sense at all).

Pain as Punishment for Sexual Guilt

One attractive, successful professional woman amazed her friends by marrying a physically powerful construction worker. She had been educated abroad in some of the finest European finishing schools and, in addition to a career as a lawyer, had written several successful novels under another name. She had been married twice previously to men whose backgrounds were similar to hers and both marriages had ended in divorce.

When friends came to the house for cocktails or a dinner

party, her newest husband often lounged around in dungarees and T-shirt, not saying much but drinking heavily. One night, in front of a group of her friends, she said to him, "How about bringing in another bottle of soda from the kitchen?"

He wheeled on her, slapped her across the face and snarled, "I'm not your God-damned servant."

She turned to her guests, a happy smile on her face and said, "I've got me a real man."

She informed an intimate friend that this husband was the only one of the three she found physically satisfactory. "I don't understand it," she said. "The others were so much closer to me in every way. They waited on me, they were polite and gentle, but they bored me. When I looked at my second husband, I wanted to vomit. He was no man. But this one is the greatest, in bed. He bites me and slaps me and punches me," and she gave an ecstatic shiver.

She continued, "Once he gave me such a black eye I had to wear dark glasses for a week. Another time my jaw swelled up so, I thought he had broken it. But I love him. The trouble with educated men is that they don't know how much a woman enjoys a good beating every now and then."

There is a widely held belief that a certain amount of masochism is natural in the female. This theory holds that female masochism is biologically based, in that the first sexual experience of the woman, because of her intact hymen, is usually painful, and the end product of sexual intimacy, childbirth, despite all modern advances, still entails a certain amount of pain. Adherents of this theory also point to the pleasure some women seem to take in discussing their operations.

But when masochism becomes as extreme as in the case of the woman above, there are usually other reasons for it. She was trying to defend her attitude as typical of all women which it obviously is not. She had been raised by a very fanatical father who rarely paid attention to her except when he was vexed and then he would slap her or pull her ears. She grew up feeling that attention from men had to be violent to be meaningful, which is often a child's view of sex even when he has not been mistreated by a parent.

Some women need to be treated brutally by their sexual partners as punishment for the guilt they feel about sexual intimacy. It is rare for a girl to be raised without repeated warnings about the undesirability of sexual activity before marriage. It is difficult for most women to shed guilt feelings completely just because a wedding ring is slipped on the third finger of her left hand. Some authorities believe this guilt is one of the chief factors preventing a number of women from enjoying their sexual experiences to the fullest. Others believe the guilt is derived primarily from secret sexual feelings for the parent of the opposite sex.

The alternative to warning a girl against indulging in sexual intimacy before marriage is not so-called complete freedom, which is bound to invoke even more guilt, but the basing of sexual education on a rational acceptance of enlightened self-interest. The girl will be far happier in the long run if she waits for the man she loves. If she is promiscuous she will lose respect for herself. The fact is that sex, deprived of any restraints, becomes a pleasureless, mechanical form of dreary calisthenics rather than a deep emotional relationship. There may be the moment of relief of tension but it may be followed by many moments of self-hatred.

Some young men and women, raised by parents who thought they were being permissive when they were really uncaring, engage in frenetic sexual relations of shortlived duration on a kind of round-robin basis, an empty and unsatisfying procedure. They may resort to extreme measures of sadism and masochism in an effort to impart some excitement to an activity which has become dull and routine, some even turning to drugs to try to whet an easily jaded appetite.

The Fantasy of Rape

A number of masochistic women never act out a wish to be hurt but content themselves with fantasies and dreams. One prominent fantasy is that of rape, in which the woman is brutally taken against her will and responds to this assault with a mixture of pleasure and pain. The fear of rape hides the wish for rape, a wish so intense it cannot emerge as such directly into the conscious but explodes in the reverse form of fear.

Some women who fear rape dress in particularly provocative fashion and act seductively, yet refuse to make good on their implied sexual promise. They are hoping to find a man who will refuse to take "no" for an answer but will be so overwhelmed with desire for them that he will throw off all restraints and rape them. In this way, the woman avoids taking responsibility for her sexual desire. If she is overpowered by a man, she need not feel guilty about her wishes. She was merely the innocent victim.

The Torturing Sadist

Masochistic women could not exist without sadistic men. Here, too, some authorities believe that a certain amount of sadism is natural to a male as masochism is to a woman. They point to the animal kingdom where coitus is frequently accompanied by biting, as for example, in the mating of cats. But the extreme of sadism, found in men who can make love only after beating women either emotionally or physically or both, is usually a result of poor emotional development.

One cause of sadistic behavior in males is the fear they harbor toward women. Raised by demanding, aggressive mothers, taught by punitive female schoolteachers, repulsed and ridiculed by teen-age feminine teasers, such men have great anxiety about approaching women sexually. By using brute strength, or by ripping the woman apart with harsh or dirty words, they degrade her and then feel more competent to deal with what to them has been a fearful object. Beautiful women, because of their greater capacity to arouse feelings of inadequacy among men, often tend to be the special recipients of these far from tender attentions. The most attractive girl in the crowd will, many times, wind up with the worst bounder. He ridicules her and taunts her, yet he is the one she is likely to choose from a host of admiring swains.

Some men torture their wives emotionally in a series of subtle ways. Sometimes the torture also proves painful to the man himself. The husband who arouses his wife to a pitch of intense sexual passion and then leaves her unsatisfied, time after time, may consciously feel regret at not being able to gratify his wife but may unconsciously, as revealed by psychoanalytic studies, be using this as a form of exquisite torture for both of them.

Uncontrolled sadism is a form of immaturity. Children often act like savages. They have to be taught to control their cruel impulses. It is not unusual for a child to kill small creatures like bugs without a qualm of conscience, or to strike a brother and sister ferociously, as though to kill.

The one who finds he cannot control his need to inflict pain on someone else has to face the fact that he is the victim of inner conflicts which prevent him from developing a tender, satisfactory relationship with anyone. He suffers from this uncontrolled sadistic impulse in some ways even more than the recipient of his attack, for the loneliness created by his driving away any possible closeness with someone through his brutality is frequently more difficult to bear than the actual experience of physical pain. He also must cope with the guilt of being the aggressor, while the one who receives pain is assuaging guilt through the punishment received.

The mature person possesses both sadistic and masochistic impulses, for what lies in one person lies in everyone to some degree, but he also possesses the control necessary to prevent himself from acting on such impulses. He knows he does not have to follow through on his every wish.

Repression May Cripple Reason

One need not be burdened with guilt about impulses or fantasies. Problems in relationships become serious only when these impulses are acted out or denied. If they are faced and accepted as natural, they may then be used constructively. The trouble comes when we cannot accept them and must repress them into the unconscious. If the repression becomes too intense, our unconscious cannot cope with it and the feel-ings overwhelm the conscious which is then unable to reason if too crippled.

We see this—the unconscious laid bare—in some of our mentally ill, where the conscious control has been blasted away by the intensity of the repressions. Our unconscious is not very different from the unconscious of those in mental hospitals. It is just that we are able to control our wild feel-ings and use them wisely, a process known as civilization.

The woman who finds herself involved with men who treat her cruelly, emotionally or physically, or both, should rec-ognize that this repetition is not purely fortuitous. She is probably searching for this sort of treatment from a man. It gratifies her masochistic needs and, at the same time, enables her to feel contempt for the partner who thinks he is being dominating but is only gratifying her wish for such behavior. She can feel scornful of his lack of control and at the same time enjoy the violence.

Masochism, as well as sadism, is designed to enhance loneliness for it is impossible, when masochism gets out of hand, to create any satisfactory marriage. No one loves an eternally suffering creature. They may pity, but pity is far from love as those who marry out of pity soon find out. Pity is, in large part, identifying with the suffering man or woman, and this is not a wise reason for choosing a mate.

Some men are notoriously deficient in their ability to express tenderness. Filled with anxiety about their masculinity, they fear that to be tender is somehow to be feminine. The man secure in his maleness need not show it in caricatured form by slapping women around. He can afford to be gentle and tender without feeling that his masculinity is compromised.

Similarly, some women in their envy of what they consider the superiority of the male, unconsciously try to be like men and give up their inherent female characteristics of warmth and tenderness in an attempt to act like Marine sergeants. Such women, in their aping of men, may sometimes adopt a love-'em and leave-'em philosophy, glorying in their one-night stands, and considering the man who acts sentimental and romantic as mawkish and feminine. Such women often use sex only as a means of demonstrating to the man his own inadequacy as a love partner, and they soon abandon him. The prostitute and call girl are unconsciously very envious of the man, and each act of sex in their unconscious holds in it elements of castration.

The Need To Castrate

Some wives also are guilty of wishing to emasculate their husbands. One woman gave her husband a detailed criticism of all his failings as a lover and how poorly he compared to the man whose mistress she was before marriage, which is one way of emasculating. Sometimes this need to castrate the man shows itself in frigidity when the woman refuses to have an orgasm in order not to give him the satisfaction of feeling that he is a competent male. This is not by any means the only cause of frigidity, which has many, many causes, as does any extreme behavior, but some women seem actually to glory in their frigidity and their husband's inability to satisfy them instead of being anguished by it.

When one husband developed a technique of satisfying his wife during sexual intimacy, she turned to him after an orgasm and snapped, "That was very sneaky," as though she had been determined not to have the orgasm and his causing her to experience one constituted a veiled attack. This same woman, on a subsequent occasion when she had an orgasm well before her husband, said angrily, "You beat me again." She considered her ability to have an orgasm as a defeat even though previously she complained that her husband would usually leave her unsatisfied.

Sex to her was a battlefield from which she could emerge the victor only by paying the price of her own lack of satisfaction. Here we see how intimately connected are masochism and sadism—one has been called the opposite side of the coin of the other. Wherever one is present, the other lurks underneath, in the same person. Thus, this woman expressed her sadism by attempting to deny her husband the pleasure of her gratification and at the same time expressed her masochism by denying herself the right to gratification and then complaining about it.

A similar but more extreme example is found in women who marry impotent men. One woman thought marriage would stop her from being promiscuous. Her husband refused even to try to have sexual intimacy after two weeks of marriage. She lived with him in suffering for two years before she could break away, punishing herself for her promiscuous feelings by denying herself all sexual intimacy as she endured life with a man who would not touch her.

It is interesting how often a nymphomaniac will marry a homosexual. This, too, has many reasons including the woman's unconscious fear, one she cannot admit to herself, of her sexual feelings for women from which she tried to escape in the past by having many men as denial of the fear. Often these women are really searching for the nurturing they missed from their mothers, hoping to get from the men what they failed to obtain from the mother.

Some women marry men who are precariously potent and whom they unconsciously strive to make completely impotent. One wife constantly interrupted the love-making of her husband with a variety of excuses, telling him he should take a shower, or that there was a program she wanted to watch on television, or complaining that she was tired and wanted to rest. She timed these interruptions so that it was difficult not to realize their intent, as they usually occurred just before he reached his orgasm. He then usually became so furious that he was unable to have another erection that night. Having helped to make him impotent, the wife then had the dubitable pleasure of taunting him for his impotence and exulting in the pain of suffering from her lack of gratification.

Here again, sadism and masochism are inextricably intertwined. The sadist is at heart a masochist, and the masochist, a sadist, as they act out the opposite role for each other's unconscious enjoyment. The masochist would like to inflict pain but dares not, the lesser of two evils being for him to suffer it. The sadist conquers his great fear of pain by trying to inflict the suffering he feels will be meted out to him, the lesser of his two evils.

Some men frustrate their wives by suddenly stopping sexual advances just as they both become aroused, or by premature ejaculation, a way of withholding pleasure from the wife, just as some wives will halt husbands in the middle of sexual intimacy. This is often the result of hostility, or the result of fear.

The one who finds himself living with a mate who is unsatisfactory sexually, rather than heaping abuse upon the mate whom he must take responsibility for having chosen, should search within himself in order to discover what desperate, unhappy need of his own is being met through the torture of an unfulfilled sexual life.

In each unhappy situation, it is helpful to find out how we have sought or contributed to the unhappiness if we want it to disappear. Unless we know our own part in it, we can expect nothing but the same agony over and over, no matter with whom we live.

9 THE EMPTY MARRIAGE

Some marriages start out with an illusory air of exaltation only to decline swiftly into appalling emptiness. Each partner is devastated because the act of marriage has not brought the happiness of which he dreamed.

Such people feel like the "hollow men" of Eliot's poem of the same name. Disappointed, enraged, they seek to fill the hollowness in ways that are destructive to themselves as well as to the marriage.

Promiscuity is one method of trying to avoid the emptiness. It is a way taken by some men and women as escape from facing their inner feelings.

They are victims of their own emptiness. We cannot say they are victims of society, whether they are rich and must fill leisure hours or poor and become prostitutes or pimps, supposedly because they are in need of money. We are victims of our impulses. Some authorities believe that society comes out of us and reflects our needs, while others maintain that the relation between man and society is an interactive one—man both creates and is created by the society in which he lives.

One pretty young woman of twenty-six named Frieda, living in a gilded Detroit suburb, presents a beautiful, carefully drawn mask to the world. Her hair is always a tribute to the art of hairdressing, dyed a bright gold and coiffed in the latest style. Her face, pretty enough to begin with, is enhanced by the hour or two she spends every morning meticulously applying a vast array of cosmetics, including hormone-bearing creams, royal jelly lotions robbed from thousands of deserving queen bees, delicately blended eye shadow, underliners, and eyebrow pencils, all used to mold the lovely mask.

Make-up session over, she takes to the telephone. She calls one of her many female confidantes to discuss either her husband's lastest affair or her own most recent romance. She, in turn, plays the role of listener to several of her similarly masked friends.

When involved in an extramarital romance, Frieda depends on the cooperation of one of her "girl friends," just as she has frequently aided them. This cooperation has many practical aspects. First, there is preparation of an alibi so that an afternoon spent with the club's golf pro at a nearby motel is accounted for as a shopping expedition with the friend. Then, since she does not wish to be seen in public with her current lover, Frieda must arrange to meet him at the designated rendezvous, a motel or "cheat joint," the upstairs room over some small, unsavory restaurant. But there might be danger that her car would be spotted in one of these sordid spots, so she exchanges cars with a friend completely above reproach at the time of the assignation, who perhaps would be lunching that day in the city with her husband. Sometimes three or four exchanges are necessary to evade suspicion.

After the rendezvous, Frieda spends a day or two in extensive post-mortems with her frends, enjoying a mild anxiety as to whether or not her husband has sensed her latest escapade. She admits the affairs themselves hold little meaning or pleasure for her. The pleasure lies in the danger of the forbidden, in the manipulation, in the excited discussions afterwards with her friends. She experiences her life, except for these episodic intrigues, as an empty pit.

"What else should I do?" she asks, with a shrug of her seductive shoulders. "Go crazy with boredom?"

Her husband is similarly involved in affair after affair. They try to keep the knowledge of their transgressions from each other but each is well aware as to what the other is up to, although they never openly confront each other with any accusations. They do not want to lose what they have at home, even though it does not satisfy completely.

The Falseness of Frenetic Excitement

Frieda is typical of a number of her exurbanite sisters who have led lives devoid of the acceptance of frustration, who are unable to postpone the slightest pleasure. She is the only daughter of a doting father who worked very hard all his life amassing money so he could give the apple of his eye "everything she ever wanted." When she was a child, her mother carefully planned activities so Frieda would have a constant round of excitement. Her father tried to gratify all her whims, whether it was a new dress, a horse, membership in a golf club, or permitting her to leave a school that was too difficult. At twelve, she refused to remain in a summer camp because the counsellors were "mean" to her, their meanness consisting of requiring her to make her own bed.

Never having been given the opportunity of mastering frustration or being required to work hard to earn something she desired, Frieda now has little capacity to apply herself to

any task save that of making herself more beautiful and fulfilling her own sexual need any time she wishes with whom-
ever she wishes. The result is a feeling of emptiness so deep
that nothing ever eases it beyond a momentary respite, but
which she attempts to fill by many affairs, resulting in a life
that resembles a cross between tragic soap opera and *Forever
Amber*. Lacking an inner excitement, the kind that stems
from fulfilling one's own capacities, she grabs at a synthetic
excitement that will make her somehow feel she is alive, at
least for the moment.

A number of the members of Frieda's social set are sexually
involved with each other, leading to a complicated tangle of
past and present affairs so that at every social gathering many
are simultaneously acting a part in an ongoing little drama
and carefully observing their friends in a similar drama.

Much of the satisfaction of this group comes from first preparing for, and later conducting elaborate post-mortems
about the Saturday night dances at the country club. While
Frieda describes these dances as "loads and loads of fun,"
to the impartial observer they appear more like dreary, compulsive ritual with remarkable little variation from week to
week and year to year.

The "crowd" gathers at a table in the clubhouse where,
characteristically, the women all sit together, apart from the
men, and talk about clothes, difficulties with maids and cooks,
or more animatedly, their latest romances. The men are more
apt to speak of the state of their corporations or banks or law
offices and occasionally to discuss national or international
affairs but chiefly as to what economic effect they are having
on their own specific businesses or professions.

After an hour or so of talk, Frieda gets restless and heads
for the bar which is usually, by then, crowded, smoky, and
noisy. To a completely sober person the cacophony of voices

and orchestra is so loud as to be torturous. By now, though, Frieda is beyond caring about mere noise, for she is on the prowl, busy trying to make "contacts" for illicit meetings later in the week.

Some of the less attractive women in the crowd, in their desperate search for men, will become quite aggressive and approach a man with the romantic subtlety of a sailor in port after six months at sea. Thus, one of Frieda's friends will assail a man at the bar with the challenge, "I'll bet you're good in bed."

The men in this set, in large part the sons of domineering fathers who have been captains of industry, possess enough doubts about their masculinity to rise frequently to the bait. One of their prime reasons for getting involved in these affairs seems to be so the women can then cast them off with disparaging remarks, as though to prove their original doubts about their own masculinity.

On spying a former lover, Frieda said to him, "I wonder if you're still as poor a performer in bed as you used to be." It often seems as if these women must demonstrate that no man of their acquaintance is really an adequate male.

Another value of such affairs appears to be that the women can then get together and compare notes. Sometimes three or four will discuss a mutual lover's weaknesses and habits. It is almost as if two or three women, having had an affair with the same men, or men they all at least know, now possess a bond between them in this subject for detailed discussion. They are like children who band together secretly and in hushed, eager voices tell each other what they have seen through a keyhole as they peeked into their parents' bedroom.

The behavior of Frieda and her friends seems unpardonable to most adults but perhaps those who criticize would be more sympathetic if they observed the occasional expressions of fear and anguish that flash across the faces of these men and women in unguarded moments. Their frantic search for excitement is a vain attempt to hide from themselves the essential emptiness and loneliness of their lives.

As one man told Frieda, "I feel you've got a void in you that I couldn't possibly fill." He had sensed her insatiability.

Work as Escape from Emptiness

People fight emptiness in marriage in many ways other than promiscuity. The husband who must work twenty hours a day without much real satisfaction may also be trying to deny an inner emptiness. Such men literally spend day after day coping with the minutiae of their jobs which might better be left to a clerk, or undertaking far more work than any one mortal could handle, in order to keep themselves occupied so they can avoid facing their deeper feelings.

One such businessman hired a skilled writer to compose a twenty-page brochure. As it was being written, he revised and corrected every word in it so that the job, instead of taking a week, became a three-months project. But for these three months he was constantly occupied making notes, working overtime, and taking sections of the brochure home with him so he could work at night and into the early hours of the morning.

It was as though he had assigned himself "busy work," as teachers do to prevent children from getting into mischief. Keeping occupied with many such projects also gave him the perfect excuse for not having to satisfy his wife's sexual needs. He could always say regretfully, "I'm so tired, dear," and imply he was working so hard in order to feed her and the children.

Men such as this, to whom work has become an addictive

drug designed to lessen the pain of existence, are not to be confused with those who find in their work a true challenge and creative experience, who enjoy what they do yet also manage to find time to spend with their families.

Some couples fight the joint emptiness that surrounds them by possessing one interest in common and it suffices for a short period of time. One woman told a friend that the only thing that "kept her alive" was the nightly visits to the local harness race track where both she and her husband would wager small sums of money. It was the one place they found each other companionable. Like many compulsive gamblers, they used betting as a way of pumping up in themselves a feeling of excitement lacking in the rest of their life.

One of the most common ways of trying to combat emptiness is to resort to the excessive use of alcohol. Here, the essential inability of empty people to express feeling becomes clear, for many alcoholics confess that the only time they feel free to give way to emotion is when under the influence of alcohol. The man who is filled with deep resentment against women, and most particularly his wife, frequently cannot express it at all except when drunk. Then he is able to give vent to it not only verbally but often physically as well. This is one of the reasons for the prevalence of drunken beatings.

The wives of alcoholic men are a fascinating study in themselves. A recent survey shows that such women may go through years of suffering at the hands of an alcoholic husband and remain strong as long as their husbands drink, but if the husband becomes cured, the wives often sink into serious depressions. They seem to need a problem husband in order to fill their own emptiness with his difficulties. While they can care for him or worry about him, they are able to forget their own lack of emotional fullness.

Also, a drunken husband may be acting out rebellion and

anger that his wife secretly wishes she were able to express and she gets a vicarious thrill out of his violence. Quite often an overly sweet, patient, submissive woman will marry a man who is an alcoholic. This is no accident. He is serving a purpose in her unconscious life, as is she in his.

Sometimes tough economic going and the husband's inability to provide adequately for the family serves the same function as his alcoholism to a wife. Some of the women in Frieda's crowd refrained from becoming promiscuous as long as their husbands struggled to establish themselves financially. The success of the husband seemed to have proved unsettling, because as long as they did not have much money, the wives were able to consider their lack of emotional resources purely a lack of financial resources, but when they possessed money and had to admit the void still existed, they then took to promiscuity as an escape.

Rather than resort to trying to escape emptiness in ways that are futile and only result in intensifying it, pushing one further into lonely despair, those who find their lives meaningless would be far happier if they searched within themselves for the causes, even if they needed professional help in this search.

The Twentieth Century Zombie

One of the characteristics of protoplasm, the basic ingredient of all living organisms, is its irritability. In trying to prevent psychic irritation, which is the result of any painful or dangerous feeling, some turn themselves into the living dead. Trying to give themselves a deceptive quality of life, they become frantic automatons pulled back and forth by endless, superficial involvements. Fearful of experiencing the pain that true involvement brings, they are the self-made zombies of our civilization.

Boredom or mild depression is often a withdrawal of feelings—anger, fear, jealousy, sexual hunger—a refusal to face feelings felt as dangerous and painful.

A striking example of this is shown in the recent book and movie, *Psycho,* by Robert Bloch. The leading character is gripped by the urge to kill and as long as he kills, he can keep functioning. But when he is caught and has to face what he has done, he turns catatonic, not moving a muscle even to ward off a fly that walks across his nose, believing he is so gentle and nonviolent that he would not kill a fly.

Nor would he, as long as he has paralyzed himself and stopped all feeling of wanting to murder. To a degree, we all paralyze ourselves psychologically and physically, so we will not commit dangerous acts, since we no longer live like cannibals in the jungle but have the same impulses as primitive man.

Some women obtain a false sense of taking part in a life that seems to be passing them by when they become vicariously involved in their friends' activities through gossip, giving endless advice (usually unheeded) or acting as confidante. Others seek to fill their emptiness by engaging in a ceaseless round of action, joining countless organizations, or plunging ardently into careers.

These, in themselves, are not destructive goals if the need to kill time is not a desperate one, for such work can be useful both to the women and society. A mother of two adolescent children went back to college to study politics and fit herself for a career in community activities. She is now a board member of the local mental health society and an active participant in the League of Women Voters and where previously the hours hung heavy on her hands, now she fills them with her volunteer work while still caring for her children, husband, and house.

Underneath the activities of both men and women when they are frenzied ones, lies in wait a deep, agonizing depression. The frantic action is their escape from facing the depression. The depression, in turn, is caused by hidden, repressed feelings, one of the most intense of which is anger carried over from childhood.

Children cannot show much rage at their parents because they are afraid of retaliation. An angry parent is experienced as one who does not love, and children need to feel that they are loved and cared for. An angry parent can kill a child, as some actually do.

Some children are bought off by parents who "give" them everything; how can a child become angry at a parent who does everything for him? In a sense, such children are bribed into unfeelingness and boredom. Their anger, repressed, is intense because they resent their parents' substituting material things for real concern.

The Danger of Insatiability

But it must be remembered, also, that all children become angry to a certain degree when their demands, which are insatiable to start with, cannot always be met. Children must inevitably be frustrated in some way—that is the price of civilization. Often it is not what the parents did but the child's distortion of their motives. Parents could be angels and the child, when frustrated, would still think of them as malevolent.

However, the child's future life as an adult may be made more difficult by parents who, although well meaning, are afraid of losing his love and will not set the controls and limits necessary to the healthy development of his personality. Children must learn to accept the postponement of pleasure, a difficult task for them.

As we grow up, we realize we must expect a certain amount of frustration because there will be greater gain for us in the long run. Wise parents know this and help their children learn it, chiefly through setting the example and showing themselves able to tolerate frustration. Words alone are not enough, for "Do as I say, not as I do," does not work with children.

Some have used Freud as an excuse for indulging in gratification of their every sexual wish, not realizing that Freud, in common with most psychoanalysts, teaches that civilization and maturity are impossible without the postponing of much immediate gratification. Freud was the most moral of men in his own life, in his philosophy and teachings. Psychoanalysis emphasizes the importance of our being able to accept frustration if we wish to be emotionally mature. If our every wish is gratified, this converts pleasure into a vice because it then becomes an addiction.

The emotionally mature person, able to cope with frustration, thus avoids emptiness. He knows he cannot have his own way all the time. He does not expect to get it, realizing it is sheerest fantasy for him to demand that his every wish be fulfilled the second it springs to mind.

He is willing to face the feelings that might be dammed up behind boredom and depression, to examine some of the fantasies that may have intensified these feelings. He is able to separate illusion from reality and thus profit from both.

Life without fantasy would be grim indeed, and life without reality leads to madness. Each has its place and the wise person is able to enjoy both his fantasy, when he needs it, and the reality of life around him.

10 THE RESPECTABLE PROSTITUTE AND THE PROPER PIMP

There is a world of difference between giving for selfish reasons, demanding something in return, and giving for the pleasure of doing so and seeking no reward.

Those with the first attitude are apt to find life empty. If payment is expected for a gift and not received, then it is easy to feel like a martyr, choke up with self-pity, feel exploited, hate, and demand revenge.

There are some who think of love not as a gift but contracted for on the barter system—"What are you going to do for me if I promise to love you?"

The penalty for such a penurious feeling about love is twofold. Enjoyment of the other person as a full human being goes by the board when such trades are made, and the self cannot help but feel cheated in demanding the bargain for the price is never right.

One kind of bargain is made when sexual favors are traded for other than one's own pleasure. One intelligent, sensitive woman, troubled by her lack of sexual desire for her husband, feels that if she does not allow him to make love to her when-ever he requests it, he will forsake her. She submits to his demands, and, as so often happens in such a situation, she is slowly building up an ever-increasing distaste for sex because of this submission. But this is her bargain, made with herself so her husband will not abandon her. It is a question of how deep her distaste for sex and for herself will become before she will either explode at him or herself.

Another wife, whenever she has an unpleasant request to make of her husband to which she knows he will object, such as buying an expensive refrigerator or visiting relatives he finds abhorrent, will act seductively to try to make him more amenable. Some women become especially inviting when they want their husbands to give them money for an extrava-gant purchase. As one comedian puts it, "Most mink coats are sold in bed."

Such women, although perhaps not consciously aware of it, are psychologically similar to the prostitute who sells her body to get money out of a man. And, like the prostitute, they have deeper reasons for their need to do this, of which the demand for money is only a symptom. Money is rarely the whole of the story nor even the most important part of it. The prostitute often holds contempt for a man, envies him, and may unconsciously be out to destroy him.

On the other side of this *folie à deux* ("madness shared by two") stands the man who is psychologically a pimp, even though he does not actually sell his wife's body to other men. He uses her rather than enjoying her as a person. He insists she do the work around the house, raise his children, take care of him, and all this without giving very much of himself. He may occasionally engage in sexual intimacy, even as do pimps, but without love or tenderness, not desirous of his wife but only of what she can do for him.

As one wife put it, "My husband throws me an occasional crumb of sex so I will keep on taking care of him and the house."

There exists no feeling between the two of them of sharing, building, giving to each other. They will remain together as long as one or the other does not become too dissatisfied with the bargain.

The Unfulfilled Promises

A common bargain, unspoken, is sometimes made when a man or woman marries for money, promising love in return. There are men who marry for money without loving the woman (it is possible, of course, to love a woman who is wealthy). Nor are these men always poor. One man who inherited an estate of nearly a million dollars married a woman who was slated to inherit at least ten times as much. He was trained for such a marriage by his father who had always brought home to him strongly that a marriage to a rich woman would advance him socially. The marriage ended in divorce for it had little to do with affection.

Another man married the daughter of an important industrialist not so much for the money but for the powerful position this would give him in the financial empire his father-in-law had built. But instead of achieving any real power, he found himself the vassal of two tyrants, his wife and his father-in-law, from which tyranny he retreated into a series of psychosomatic ailments.

His wife demanded sexual satisfaction beyond what he felt his capacity to give, and the father-in-law would then express the intense competitiveness which had made him successful by saying scornfully of his son-in-law, "He's no man," or calling him, "an incompetent pensioner."

More usual is the woman who marries a rich man, believing that if her material wants are met she will be able to love him. When this is the main goal of marriage, the life together of husband and wife often turns out to be shallow, unfriendly, empty of tenderness. Frequently one or the other eventually seeks love elsewhere, for money is not a reliable cement for affection.

Between the real prostitute and her pimp there usually exists brutality, for this is inherent in such an abnormal relationship. When sexual feeling is perverted and used for gain it causes anger because of the loss of real satisfaction. In lesser degree, brutality will often erupt in a marriage that is made as a bargain.

A woman who purchases a man usually holds an underlying contempt for him because he has allowed himself to be bought. The man reacts to this contempt, which only mirrors the contempt he feels for himself, by retaliating with anger and brutality, usually psychological, but sometimes also physical.

One man married a woman who became very successful in a modeling career and encouraged him to stay home and write, although there was no evidence that he possessed much creative ability. She seemed to need to prove that he was incapable of taking care of her. He retaliated by insulting her at dinners and parties, deriding comments she made about topics of general interest, and complaining publicly about how badly she managed the home. The marriage has lasted although neither is particularly happy, because his need to be dependent meshes neurotically with her need to prove no man can take care of her financially. She had a father who always failed to earn enough money to support his family and this has been part of her image of man.

The Wish Is Father to the Deed

Some mothers, in essence, train their daughters to be respectable prostitutes by constantly warning, "Don't throw yourself away on a poor man," or "Don't give in to a man sexually unless he shows he cares for you by giving you presents." Some encourage their daughters to be seductive in order, first, to be socially successful, and later, materially successful.

One mother, when she became concerned because her daughter at sixteen went out on fewer dates than her classmates, rebuked her, saying, "You're too much of a prude. You've got to learn to lead the boys on."

Another remarked to her eighteen-year-old daughter, kidding on the square, as they say, "What are you saving it for?" It is not surprising that today her daughter, at the age of twenty-three, is quite a promiscuous young woman.

Such mothers are encouraging their daughters to act out their own secret impulses to be promiscuous. A number of wives who outwardly lead lives of rigorous respectability are perched on volcanoes of intense voluptuous desires. One way in which they sometimes communicate this to their daughters is to constantly inveigh against the daughter's own expression of physical desire, thereby planting in the daughter's mind this method of rebellion.

One college student of nineteen would be asked sarcastically by her mother after every date, all of which were quite innocent at the beginning, "Well, did you go to a motel or use the back seat of the car?"

Eventually the daughter did become promiscuous, telling a friend, "Since mother thinks I'm this way anyhow, I might as well enjoy myself. I've got the name—why not the game?" She was now indulging her impulses, rather than controlling them, because she felt this was one way of getting even with her mother for what had started out as unfounded accusations, as well as at a deeper level acting out her mother's unconscious wishes which expressed themselves in the sarcastic comments.

Similarly, sometimes because of their own suppressed sexual desires, fathers will question or taunt daughters and sons with suspicion and distrust. If a parent never demonstrates trust in a child, it is difficult for that child to develop trust in himself or anyone else. Parents who are not able to trust children are often not able to trust themselves.

Another kind of example showing fear taken as a command occurred in the running of the Kentucky Derby in 1957. Just before the race, Ralph Lowe, owner of the horse Gallant Man, was talking with his jockey William Shoemaker. Lowe described a dream he had had the night before in which Bill had mistaken the sixteenth pole for the finish line and stood up on the horse just before the end of the race.

Later, at the actual running of the race, Bill was ahead on Gallant Man at the end of a mile and three-sixteenths, with one more sixteenth to go. Suddenly he stood up, appearing to hold back his horse. With less than a sixteenth of a mile remaining, he could not make up the tiny fraction of ground lost and Iron Liege forged ahead and won the race.

Afterward, Bill confessed he had mistaken the last sixteenth pole for the finish line, just as in Mr. Lowe's dream. Unconsciously, Bill had taken as an order Mr. Lowe's warning not to stand up on the horse, expressed as a fear in the dream, just as children often take warnings as an order to do exactly what the parent forbids.

The man who may act somewhat like a pimp in his marriage, expecting to give little for what he receives, is often the result of a childhood in which he may have been over-protected and excessively cared for by a mother who continued to treat him as an infant even when he grew up. He expects from all women the same overindulgence and the right to evade his responsibility in the relationship, as he did as a child with his mother.

The Fascination of Prostitution

A question that many moral women ask themselves is, "What would it feel like to be a prostitute?" This wayward, abandoned, socially degrading life holds the fascination of the morbid and forbidden, and the so-called "prostitution fantasy" is not uncommon among women of all social ranks.

A delicate, lovely model who grew up in a deeply religious family, became greatly distressed when, finding sexual intimacy with her husband bitterly unfulfilling, she would constantly daydream about picking up gross, ugly men, whom she described as "the truck driver type with dirty fingernails and bloated beer bellies," and allowing them to become intimate with her under the boardwalk at Coney Island for fifty cents apiece.

The prostitute fantasy arises in part from the inability of a number of properly brought up women to combine the tender, loving feelings they developed in the bosom of their family with the sexual desires that become powerful during adolescence. Since as girls they were taught that sex is forbidden, dirty and degrading, the only way they can dream of sexual fulfillment is under forbidden, dirty and degrading circumstances, or where they become the innocent victim of the sadistic man and need take no responsibility for the act.

To some women, to be sexual at all is the same as being a prostitute. One who had reached her late thirties without a sexual experience was discussing with a friend the man with whom she had finally fallen in love.

"Why don't you sleep with him?" suggested the friend.

The woman drew back in horror. "Do you want me to become a prostitute?" she said in alarm.

To her, to accept and act on her normal sexual feelings was the equivalent of being a prostitute.

Similarly, some married women will say of their husbands' sexual desires which they feel excessive, "He really wants a prostitute."

Men who have been brought up to overevaluate and deify women, when faced with their wife's sexual desire may think, "She's nothing but a prostitute at heart," unable to accept the woman's need to fulfill a natural appetite.

Sexual Feelings Are Natural and Necessary

One reason we may feel sex degrading and forbidden is that the first place we experienced sexual feelings is in the house where we grew up, and there sex *was* forbidden and often labeled degrading, especially any thought of sexual desire for a parent or brother or sister, which was particularly repugnant and repulsive.

It is now recognized as natural to feel some sexual attraction for the parent of the opposite sex when we are growing up, for such attraction between daughter and father, or son and mother, is then available for transfer to a husband or wife later on.

In families where all sexual feeling is deeply repressed, it is difficult for the children in later life to accept these sensual feelings, for they feel their sexual desire as something wicked, not something to which every human being is entitled. Such children do not realize that incestuous feelings need not be acted upon, just accepted. When children are given love and understanding, the physical yearning for the parent of the opposite sex is usually transferred more easily in later life to someone outside the family.

If a child grows up with parents who have more than their share of emotional problems, he may experience intense feelings for the parent of the opposite sex, sometimes provoked by the parent, and then feel a deep guilt because of these feelings. The guilt may become so strong it interferes with his ability to mature emotionally and he remains fixed, sexually, at an early level. He is then unable to harness his erotic feelings to his entire growth but instead holds them to this primitive level out of his deep attachment to the parent and his fear of losing the parent should he express affection for anyone else. This is considered by some to be one of the causes of homosexuality and Lesbianism, both the man and the woman unable to break free of a deep attachment to the mother.

Most mature persons, at one time or another, realize they must give up their early childhood desire to "marry" the parent of the opposite sex. Otherwise they may be in emotional trouble all their lives. No matter how brutal, how selfish the parent, apparently many children feel this sexual attraction to the parent of the opposite sex although it is often not conscious but expresses itself in disguised form in dreams and fantasies.

If we are able to accept that it was natural for us as children to have a certain amount of warm feelings for the parent of the opposite sex, then with guilt out of the way, we will probably be better able to feel both tender and sensuous toward a husband or wife and love will not have to be bestowed as a bargain, but may more likely be given willingly as a gift.

11 THE UNFAITHFUL

Each one likes to think of himself as faithful after his own fashion. Even the husband or wife who transgresses often rationalizes his waywardness so that he feels faithful to his mate. The high percentage of unfaithfulness in marriage that Kinsey and his collaborators discovered in their study of American sexual behavior proved disturbing to our image of ourselves.

While there has been considerable criticism of the validity of the Kinsey figures as applied to the population of the nation as a whole, we must consider seriously the fact that 50 per cent of married men are unfaithful at some time in their lives as compared to 26 per cent of married women.

Despite the disparity in these percentages, with husbands much more frequently unfaithful than wives, most people reacted with greatest shock to the revelation of female unfaithfulness. All their new-found equality notwithstanding, women apparently have not yet gained the sanction to be as unfaithful in marriage as men. Madame Bovary is still an outcast.

Unfaithfulness seems a simple enough concept. But what is it?

It is remarkable how subjective the definition of unfaithfulness is to most people. There are women who become torn by guilt and consider themselves unfaithful hussies when they even look admiringly for a fleeting moment at any man other than their husbands, believing it a sign of wantonness merely to think of another man sexually. At the other extreme are those who do not consider themselves unfaithful even if they engage in affairs, as long as their husband remains innocent of their sexual flings and thus, they believe, unhurt.

Some are so obsessed with the feeling of guilt at having desired another man that, since they consider the great sin to be the mere wanting, they will allow the man to make love to them because they feel there is little difference between desiring and consummation. This may be a form of rationalization so they may justify an impulse they do not wish to control.

The wish is not the deed. Almost every human being at some time in his life may want to kill someone, but there is the greatest of differences between the wish and the act, as borne out by the consequences, which are so different.

Similarly, almost every married person, no matter how much in love he may be, will at one time or another be stirred sexually by somebody other than his mate. If he can accept this as part of the natural wish for novelty, he need not feel torn by guilt at the wish, nor need he act on what is usually only a transient impulse.

What Is Unfaithfulness?

The definition of unfaithfulness is complicated by what degree of intimacy is considered unfaithful. Some believe flirting at a party is a marked sign of unfaithfulness either in themselves or their mate. Among certain groups, kissing between men and women as a form of greeting is as innocent as a handshake, while in others such a kiss would be considered flagrant violation of the marriage vow.

Some women will indulge in long and ardent petting sessions with a strange man but draw the line at final intimacy because they feel that only the ultimate step constitutes unfaithfulness. One married woman is even willing to satisfy men other than her husband orally but will not engage in intercourse which she feels would produce too much guilt for her to handle, although many of us would consider oral sex more intimate than conventional intercourse.

Possibly unfaithfulness is a combination of two things— how the husband or wife feels about it and how his or her mate feels. One wife, watching her husband flirt mildly with a pretty dinner partner, was happy to see him enjoying himself. Another wife, every time her husband even talked to an attractive woman at a party, became violently jealous and later accused him of wanting to have an affair with the woman.

The attitudes produced in the husbands by these two wives were entirely different. The husband of the first woman loved her all the more for her understanding and felt no need to become further involved with any woman. The husband of the second woman became enraged at her accusations and they would fight bitterly for days on end.

The first wife felt rather confident of her attractiveness as a woman so she could afford to be tolerant of her husband's mild interest in another woman, not needing to possess his every smile and glance. The second wife felt so insecure about her own desirability that she had to engage in constant surveillance of her husband's behavior, ready to repel the attack of other women to whom she felt inferior, ready to resent his slightest interest in another woman as a threat to their marriage.

A third wife, aware of her husband's flirtatiousness, would promptly set out to be friendly and charming to any woman on whom he showered attention. She hoped to be able to arouse the woman's conscience enough so she would fend off any further advances her husband might make.

Some wives, upon seeing their husbands show the slightest interest in another woman, will then flirt with the nearest man. One woman, married for three years, became highly overwrought when she discovered her husband had lunched with a former sweetheart. She promptly called an unmarried woman friend and arranged to go out with her on a double date. Even though she found her blind date completely without charm, she let him fondle her and then went home and taunted her husband, telling him what she had done.

Her need to retaliate was so intense that she could not bear the thought of permitting his insult, as she saw the luncheon, to go unavenged even though, as it turned out, her husband's date had been an innocent one and had resulted in no further meetings.

Some weigh unfaithfulness in terms of quantity, not quality, forgiving one indiscretion but not ten or fifteen. Yet unfaithfulness is an attitude, not a number. A man may be unfaithful only once but it may be more disastrous to his marriage than if he were unfaithful fifty-two times a year.

Causes of Infidelity

What are the causes of unfaithfulness? Why do men and women who say they want to maintain their marriage seek sexual intimacy outside of marriage, thus courting the danger of destroying the marriage?

One reason for unfaithfulness may be an unexpressed anger at the mate. One husband, each time he became furious at his wife, would say nothing to her but go out and pick up a strange woman and have intercourse with her. This behavior of his was so regular that he recognized it as compulsive. Only when he was able to express hostility directly to his wife and she was able to understand the reasons for his wrath, did he stop needing other women. He was receiving psychiatric help and, as a result, also came to realize that much of his anger at his wife had been unfounded.

Another reason for unfaithfulness given by some is boredom. One woman, discovered by her husband in a compromising situation with another man in a beach cabana, wailed to a friend, "If only I'd been able to arrange a card game for the afternoon, the whole thing wouldn't have happened. I had nothing to do and he happened by." Boredom, as discussed previously, is often a rationalization hiding many other feelings.

Some are unfaithful because they need reassurance of their sexual prowess. The married Don Juan may possess serious doubts about his masculinity, his potency, or his attractiveness to the opposite sex, and attempt to dispel these doubts by engaging in endless short-lived sexual adventures in an effort to prove he is attractive, potent, and desirable. It is quite difficult for some men to demonstrate their potency in these affairs because Don Juans often are the victims of such severe sexual anxiety as rarely to be fully potent with any woman.

This is also true of the nymphomaniac, for no matter how many men she is intimate with during her lifetime, she never truly feels like a woman. She is in constant search of her femininity as she asks man after man to reassure her of it through their temporary possession of her.

Underneath the need for reassurance through promiscuity

in both sexes may lurk a deep fear of homosexuality. Promiscuity is a common defense against admitting one's feelings for members of the same sex, feelings that are natural when they exist in moderate degree, for they permit the forming of friendships, but which may be felt as dangerous if they are intense or denied.

One man who frequently, to his own disgust, felt impelled to go to a prostitute even though he was married to a woman he found desirable, realized that his visits to prostitutes followed close upon the heels of each meeting with a male friend who aroused vague, disturbing feelings in him. It is no accident that, after long hours devoted exclusively to masculine company, such as a poker game or a convention, some men feel the need to end the night by going together to prostitutes or arranging for call girls to come to their hotel rooms. It is as if they were denying the possible homosexual implications of spending time in exclusively male company by rushing off to the nearest woman who will have them.

Our youth-worshiping culture seems to make increasingly necessary the need to deny the onset of age. Through newspaper and magazine page, television and billboard, the advertising industry continuously advises men and woman to maintain their youthfulness by imbibing the proper beverages, or using the correct face creams, or wearing a certain brassiere or girdle, or dyeing the hair, or buying a toupee. The advertisements imply it is sinful for anyone, even a grandmother, to lose the natural bloom of sweet sixteen.

Men who believe they feel the start of the waning of their physical power may be galvanized into feverish activity to demonstrate they are still as virile as ever by finding a succession of women, preferably younger ones, to prove their amorous prowess is undiminished by the passing years.

Women, too, may attempt to deny what the mirror tells

them about the impact of the years, by becoming more seductive and in some cases they carry this to the point of indulging in meaningless affairs. One cynical woman in her mid-forties admitted, "Whenever I begin to feel old, I find myself a new lover."

But many a man and woman who have been happy in their marriage, who find within each other and their children all they need, accept the advancing years without complaint and discover that the serenity and contentment of older age is reward enough.

The inability to face the mature years is related to another quality frequently found among those driven within themselves to be unfaithful. They need to admire their own attractiveness. Their interest in others is chiefly a means of keeping up their esteem of themselves.

Very attractive women, accustomed to adulation, may suffer from this need to be admired constantly. Attractiveness to them is often the result not so much of natural endowment but of long and arduous preparation. This is not to imply that every woman should not do whatever she feels necessary to enhance her looks, for the emotionally mature woman takes pains to be as well groomed and attractive as possible, knowing the face she presents to the world often tells what she thinks of herself.

But if good grooming and looking attractive become the major interest of one's life, many other things will go by the board. Like Narcissus, such people tie themselves to a placid pool in which they admire their own image but never reach out for closeness with anyone else.

Some require that the pool be a person of the opposite sex who will, in word or deed, keep reflecting their beauty back to them through praises. This praise may take the form of sexual intimacy as they indulge in affairs whose only purpose is to bear temporary testimony to their attractiveness.

One woman, talking about her many lovers, complained, "What can I do? The poor dears find me so attractive they just can't control themselves," conveniently omitting to mention how seductive she would act in order to attract the "poor dears."

Illicit Sex Used as Rebellion

Another reason given for unfaithfulness is to rebel against convention. Most of us possess the impulse to react against authority, for it is one way in which we grow away from our parents and develop our own character. A certain amount of rebellion is required for our normal development. But if the authority of a parent over a child is exercised in a tyrannical manner, the rebellion of the child may become an ingrained, undeviating, furious drive which in later life may propel him into fanatic and disastrous deeds.

Some spend their lives in senseless rebellion against even the most benign of regulations. Those who hate law and order, such as the willful traffic violators, join with our delinquents in showing their defiance of authority. The world of sex, ringed as it is with such strong taboos, for such people constitutes a perfect battlefield. They leap to the barricades of sexual rebellion at every opportunity. This may be one of the reasons that rebels of all kinds are often equated in the public mind with sexual license. Perhaps there are just as many rebels who are impotent as promiscuous.

One woman, defending her love affairs outside of marriage, said defiantly, "I'm not going to be tied down by the stupid conventions of a narrow-minded society. If I need a lover to feel fulfilled, I will take one and nobody is going to stop me."

She was the daughter of parents who made many arbitrary

and contradictory demands upon her as she grew up. Rebellion seemed to thread through her life. She had married a man who she thought would be as unacceptable to her parents as she could find. When her mother, instead of railing against her choice of husband, declared he would be good for her, she then proceeded to demonstrate how bad this man was for her by having affairs with other men, about which she managed to have both husband and parents find out.

One of the ironies in such rebelliousness is that often, instead of being contrary to the parent's wishes, it turns out to be exactly what the parent unconsciously desired. This is shown in other ways than sexual unfaithfulness.

One woman married a man of a different religious faith because she "wasn't going to let my mother tell me who to marry." She then discovered that her mother also had been very much in love with a man of a different faith before her marriage and had often regretted that she had lacked the courage to follow through on her original choice. Subtly she had imparted to her daughter the desire to do what she never was able to do.

Another mother kept warning her daughter, who was very popular during adolescence, "You'd better stop running around with so many boys. You have to learn how to settle down with one." When her daughter got married, she then warned her, "Don't forget, you're married now. Don't have anything to do with any other men!"

The mother's constant warnings aroused in the daughter an interest in the possibility of becoming involved with other men, along with the wish to rebel against her mother's orders. When the daughter did indulge in an extramarital affair, she was both rebelling against her mother's overt demand that she be faithful and acting out her mother's unspoken wish that she had been unfaithful herself.

Sometimes it is the father who has himself been unfaithful who will harp on his daughter's purity because of his fear that she will follow in his footsteps. Frequently daughters are aware of a father's promiscuity, and angered by it and what they consider the hypocrisy of his demands upon them. They say in effect, "If it was good enough for father, it is good enough for me. I will be a girl just like the girls that dear old dad played around with." They caricature the father in their anger.

Repeating the Familiar

Unfaithfulness does not take place in a vacuum. There are always specific reasons why one gives in to the impulse to be unfaithful. Often a husband or wife is unconsciously imitating adults important to them in their childhood, or repeating a situation familiar to them as a child. We usually find that seemingly inexplicable behavior is due to the wish to repeat something to which we became accustomed during childhood.

One man grew up in a home where the duties of raising him were shared equally by his mother and a maiden aunt. Before marriage he was usually involved with two women at once. He never seemed able to fall in love with one woman but always was trying to decide which of two equally desirable girls he should marry. When he eventually made his decision, he was able to remain faithful to his wife for only a comparatively short time and then established a long-lasting liaison with another woman.

He denied vigorously that he did not love his wife and, similarly, that he did not love his mistress. But he could not choose between them and had to find many subterfuges so he could divide his time equally between the two. (A movie of several years ago, "The Captain's Paradise," provided an interesting variation on this theme as the captain hero spent his time ferrying between Gibraltar and North Africa, maintaining a wife in each port, devoted to each although their personalities were very different.) To solve his dilemma would probably require that he gain enough understanding to face within himself the patterns of his early life which he unconsciously kept repeating, always needing two women as he once had two mothers at his beck and call.

Another man, raised by a mother and five doting sisters, found that he always had to be the center of a group of admiring women, even after he was married. As might be expected, for the unconscious is often damnably accurate, he stopped at what was for him the magic number of six, and after five affairs outside of marriage, never again was tempted by a woman. In this case the fates conspired by presenting him with three daughters so he was able to re-establish the earlier situation of being surrounded by a bevy of adoring females.

Fear May Provoke Promiscuity

Sometimes a sudden, unexpected anxiety will provoke an otherwise faithful mate into an affair. One wife who had been scrupulously strait-laced, had never even kissed a man other than her husband, took an overseas airplane trip to join him in Paris. It was her first flight in a plane and she was frightened to death the moment they left the ground.

A strange man sitting next to her talked to her and comforted her and later she permitted him intimate caresses of a type she had never before even dreamed of with anyone but her husband. In this case, her partial unfaithfulness was an attempt to deal with the fear and anxiety she felt while in the air. Fear of death may provoke some of us to perilous acts we otherwise might not perform, and this probably accounts for much of the promiscuity that occurred among the armed troops during World War II and during every war.

One husband was faithful to his wife except when his business, due to conditions beyond his control, fell into a temporary precarious state which lasted three months, during which time he engaged in four affairs. When the business again straightened out and his anxiety lessened, he found he did not need any woman but his wife.

Love Can Listen

A humorous picture of infidelity, a cliché by now, is shown in the cartoon of a husband gazing intently into the eyes of a wide-eyed blonde and stating with apparent sincerity, "My wife doesn't understand me." Sometimes communication between husband and wife becomes so attenuated that each feels lonely and isolated even within marriage and needs to search for another companion with whom he can discuss feelings and thoughts he is unable to reveal to his mate.

One woman, married to a hard-driving executive who was always so busy with plans and projects for industrial expansion that she found it almost impossible to talk to him about anything personal, became involved with another man chiefly because he was willing to listen occasionally to whatever she wished to talk about and to share his experiences with her.

While the involvement was originally innocent enough, based on compassion and a desire to understand, they drifted into sexual intimacy, for it is difficult for most adult men and women to be united closely in a relationship without sexual overtones playing an important part.

When the husband learned of the affair, after his initial

hurt he recognized his own contribution to it and made a strong effort to give more attention to his wife so she would not have to go elsewhere to find a sympathetic ear and shoulder. It is easy for many of us, pulverized by the pressures of everyday living, to forget that those close to us need intimate communication at times. If this cannot be supplied in marriage, the need may become so great that the mate will seek outside of marriage for its fulfillment.

It is important to listen, as well as to talk. To be able to listen is part of a mature relationship. The one who talks all the time is apt to be putting on a performance rather than sharing contact with another human being. Everyone is entertained by the show-off at a party but no one wants to accompany him home and be forced to be the sole admirer. It is helpful to a marriage if we are able to listen to the dramas, hopes, and sorrows of those we love, not only out of a sense of duty or out of our own need to be loved, but listening because we deeply care for them.

One of the reasons, in addition to their inner conflicts, why people go to psychoanalysts, is to find the sympathetic ear they seem unable to locate any other place. It is a bitter commentary on our space-age civilization that many can find no one to listen to them but a psychoanalyst, and they must pay for this privilege. Psychoanalysis is far more than just being listened to, but the willingness to listen shown by the psychoanalyst plays a large part in the desire of the one who speaks to deal constructively with the emotional problems in which he may be caught.

Sex Just for the Whim of It

With some husbands and wives, there seems to be no apparent reason for the unfaithfulness. These are the obviously im-

pulse-ridden. A young woman went to a party with her husband who left early to drive home a guest who was ill. At
one point she found herself alone in a bedroom with one of
the men at the party and, without any conscious wish or intent
on her part, she suddenly was allowing him to make love to
her.

This was only one of a number of such incidents that had
happened to her. She could not explain why she indulged in
such affairs. Frequently she had only the haziest of memories
as to what had occurred, almost completely unable to describe
it. When, a year later, she met a partner in one of these epi-
sodes, she could not even remember his name and had difficulty believing him when he told her what had happened.

Such people are the victims of their unrestrained impulses.
They take no time to think over the implications of what
they do. They are apt to act on impulse in many ways, not
only sexually. As she was strolling along a pier one evening,
one married woman, who had engaged in many impulsive
affairs, looked down at the river flowing under the pilings
and suddenly jumped into the water, clothes and all.

She was rescued, and when asked why she jumped, she said,
"I don't know. I just felt like it."

"Didn't you know you might have drowned?" asked the
rescuer.

"I didn't think about anything," she said. "I just felt I
wanted to jump—that minute!"

Often such a person is the product of one of two extreme
ways of being raised. Either he was so strictly controlled as
to be denied normal gratification so that he never learned to
develop any controls of his own, or very few controls were
imposed, so he never learned to master his impulses. Sometimes parents practice both extremes, at times indulging
every whim of a child and at other times keeping all satis-

factions from him. Or one parent may overindulge, the other prohibit excessively.

Such was the situation of the son of divorced parents, whose mother, with whom he lived most of the time, was strict, refusing him even a piece of candy on the contention it was bad for his teeth, but whose father, with whom he would spend at least one day a week and summer vacation, gratified his every wish, even to buying him a horse which he rode only three times the entire year.

Reaction to Unfaithfulness

How does a mate usually react to unfaithfulness on the other's part? Most women who discover their husbands have been involved in an affair are hurt because they see this as a sign he does not love them. As one wife put it, "How could he go with such a tramp if he had any respect for me?"

Sometimes the actual feeling of the man is exactly the opposite. He feels that he respects his wife too much to subject her to what he believes are his excessive, or perhaps what he feels are abnormal, sexual demands. Having been brought up to believe that sex is a forbidden, vile expression of man's innate bestiality, he tries to be tender and respectful to his wife but turns to a woman he considers inferior for much of his sexual release. This is not to place responsibility on him alone for undoubtedly such men choose as wives women who unconsciously promote this split in their feelings.

Such men would not dream of making advances of too intimate a nature to their fiancées during courtship, but after tenderly kissing their bride-to-be good night, they may seek out a prostitute for the night. They have never managed to unite their feelings of love and tenderness with lust and sensuality.

Unable to fuse these two seemingly diverse components of normal love, they seek two different kinds of women, the respectable fiancée or wife with whom they feel tender and protective and the prostitute with whom they can yield to their animal lust without restraint.

Some women face a similar problem, finding themselves frigid with their husbands but easily excited sexually by a man who is of inferior status and with whom, therefore, they feel free to express emotions they consider vulgar and degrading. Often both men and women who experience this split between sexual and tender feelings are the result of over-severe training in the home, lacking the capacity for free, spontaneous acceptance of bodily feelings. Or else they have been brought up with too little guidance and control and can make no differentiation between love and pure physical desire.

Unfaithfulness is sometimes the result of many fantasies which are founded on the belief that love must be illicit to be exciting. As long as a relationship is forbidden, it is a thrilling one.

Illicit love holds in it, for one thing, the essence of masturbation, for it contains the erotic tinge of the first sexual act that is forbidden to all of us. Always afterwards, whatever is illicit is touched somewhat with masturbatory feeling.

Illicit love is also related to the childhood fantasy of falling in love with the parent of the opposite sex. It is considered cute when a little girl seriously informs visitors, "I'm going to marry Daddy," or a little boy says to his mother, "I'm going to be your husband when I grow up."

But if this fantasy is not given up in the interests of reality, the result may be illicit affairs after marriage, or, in some cases, as a substitute for marriage. To the woman who has an affair, although married, her husband represents the idealized father with whom sexual intimacy is forbidden, after the first flush of passion has paled and fantasy once again takes over. She then acts out the fantasy of stolen love with someone other than her husband.

She may also feel that her husband did not turn out to be the all-giving, permissive father she desired, and seek another man to satisfy this fantasy, a man with whom she can play-act at once again being the little girl snuggling close to Daddy. This also applies to the husband who in his affairs seeks, in fantasy, to hold his mother close. Wherever the forbidden is part of love, it is important to look to the Oedipal feelings, the strongest taboo of childhood, for possible explanation.

Some single girls show this pattern clearly by becoming involved in affairs with married men. The married man unconsciously may represent the father who was married to her mother. Often these girls will strive desperately to persuade the married man to leave his wife for them, feeling they would make him a more understanding, giving wife, as once they may have felt they would be a far better wife to Daddy than Mama could ever be.

Unfaithfulness is not always carried out with a member of the opposite sex. One woman married a man, had two children, then one day was shocked when her husband bluntly told her he did not wish any more sexual intimacy with her because he had become involved with a man. He wanted to remain married but continue his homosexual affair. The wife, in desperation, fled the home with her children and obtained a divorce.

Incidentally, we treat homosexuality as a crime, sending to jail men who are caught and convicted. The consensus of modern scientific opinion seems to be that homosexuality is essentially an emotional, rather than a physical or inherited, condition and may develop into heterosexuality after intensive psychological help.

One young man, a very successful commercial designer,

went to a psychiatrist because of intense feelings of loneliness. He mentioned, as a casual comment, that his sole sexual outlet was homosexuality. At the beginning of treatment he insisted his homosexuality was no problem to him since he considered it as good as, if not superior to, the heterosexual way of life, an argument often advanced by homosexuals.

But in the course of individual and group treatment that lasted a few years, it became clear to him that this defensive attitude was a thin veneer that overlay feelings of shame or inadequacy. He eventually found the courage to start dating girls, to indulge in an affair with a girl, and eventually to marry a very attractive and talented young woman. In the seven years since they have been married, he has found no need for homosexual relations and is the proud father of two children.

While some seem to emerge from extramarital affairs without too much apparent damage to the relationship with their mate, others are not able to manage such affairs without considerable harm to the marriage. Infidelity often ends in divorce. The law of many of our states reflects the seriousness of unfaithfulness as a breach by making it the one grounds for granting a divorce.

In some instances, the emotion of a mate or sweetheart may be so extreme that the betrayed partner will kill himself or the one he feels has destroyed his love, either his former lover or the rival, or both. The "unwritten law" recognizes the intensity of this feeling.

Most husbands and wives cannot help but react violently to a mate's infidelity, unless they have lost all love for the mate. There is, first, the commonly recognized blow to one's ego that occurs when the mate prefers someone else sexually. One suffers a deep sense of humiliation, and the feeling that the entire marriage is a mockery, for if the mate can become so easily intimate with someone else, what meaning did intimacy in marriage possess? The "forsaking all others" of the marriage ceremony was but an empty promise.

Some demand a divorce in the fear that this will be the next step anyhow and they would rather force the abandonment than be the one abandoned without notice. With a few, discovery of the mate's unfaithfulness arouses such deep emotional conflicts related to childhood fears of being deserted, that they are hurled into a state of temporary psychotic-like behavior.

The plea of temporary insanity sometimes made when a husband or wife falls back upon the "unwritten law" in avenging unfaithfulness, is more than mere legal strategy. It describes the disorganization of personality that may occur as a result of the infidelity.

The child abandoned by the mother may scream wildly because such desertion could mean literal death to an infant incapable of caring for himself. To some people, who as children have suffered deeply from fear of abandonment, all future abandonments are visualized just as grimly as this earliest of threats. And it seems that the very ones who suffered most in childhood seek those who they know unconsciously will abandon them, as they repeat the original trauma over and over in an effort perhaps to master it.

Side Effects of Infidelity

Even if estrangement, separation, divorce, suicide, or murder does not follow in the wake of infidelity, there are usually other deleterious effects. The one who enters into a sexual relationship outside of marriage may suffer from a depreciation of his own self-esteem. This will show itself in his feelings about himself, his mate, and his children.

Some who think they carefully cover their tracks find that, in one way or another, the mate has discovered their infidelity. So frequent is this discovery that there seems to be operating an unavowed wish for the discovery to take place. It is remarkable in how many subtle ways husbands and wives betray themselves to each other.

It may be the hint of a strange perfume, or the hackneyed lipsticked handkerchief, or a sudden, unexpected gift offered out of guilt, or a carelessly left letter, or a friend turned informer. Or perhaps the mate intuitively senses the infidelity or the one engaged in it unconsciously conveys news of it through something he says or a change in attitude.

One man, who normally trusted his wife implicitly, immediately accused her of unfaithfulness whenever he became involved in an affair. This is a psychic mechanism known as projection, in which we accuse someone else of the deed of which we are guilty, or the thought which lies in our mind, not theirs. The wife was aware of what he was doing, although she never admitted to him that she knew, since she was more interested in keeping their marriage intact than in punishing him for his infidelity.

Unfaithfulness, even if the mate should never find out about it, often has a corroding effect on the one who is guilty of it and on the relationship, an unconscious as well as conscious effect. When this is so, it then becomes a destructive act in which to engage.

Sometimes there are consequences quite different from those expected. Even if the one who transgresses succeeds in covering his tracks so completely that the transgression is not detected or even suspected, there may still be results he finds uncomfortable. One man, who believed he loved his wife to whom he had been married for eighteen years, had an affair with a secretary in his office when his wife went away for the summer. He entered upon the affair "just for fun," as a sexual fling with a younger woman.

But he found it was far from "fun" because, instead of being carefree and gay about it, the secretary made as many demands upon him as his wife who, after all, he felt, had a right to make demands. As the affair continued into the fall after his wife returned, he discovered that the keen sexual pleasure he had formerly enjoyed with his wife was greatly diminished because of his sense of guilt and had not been replaced in the clandestine relation with the secretary. He thus found it was impossible to have a relationship free of responsibility, the dream of many men who keep trying in vain to make an illusion come true.

How can a mate who wants to maintain the marriage cope with the infidelity of the other? It is difficult to expect anyone merely to accept the transgression. There is also a serious question whether this would be a healthy reaction for either.

A husband, whose wife discovered he was involved with one of her closest friends, became furious when, as he put it, "She patted me on the head and said, 'There now, don't be naughty any more.'" To him, her lack of feeling about his unfaithfulness meant she did not care for him but was content to let him support her without a show of love on either of their parts.

On the other hand, a woman who was slowly drifting into a close relationship with another man because her husband was so taken up with his work that he had little time for her, was quite pleased when he finally gave up the pretense of being civilized about it all and firmly forbade her to see the other man except when he was present. She realized then that she mattered to her husband in spite of his preoccupation with his business.

Unfaithfulness is a serious problem, both for the one who

is unfaithful and the one who feels betrayed but who may have behaved in such a fashion, consciously or unconsciously, that he drove the marriage partner into the illicit liaison. Each has made a contribution to the infidelity which is a sign of their discontent with each other, and both should examine the deed with this in mind.

If there has been unfaithfulness, the important thing to realize, for both husband and wife, is that unfaithfulness is often a symptom of a deeper conflict, and should be treated like any other symptom, by understanding the cause.

Discovery of the deeper conflicts can often preserve a marriage that would otherwise head for the psychic shoals, just as discovery of a symptom of some deep-seated physical problem can, if found in time and treated properly, save a life.

12   IS MARRIAGE FOR EVERYONE?

Love and marriage are united in our minds from childhood on. We think of one as leading inevitably to the other. But with many men and women this does not happen.

Despite the powerful pressures which society, acting through family and well-meaning friends, exerts so constantly on the unmarried, there are still millions who steadfastly hold to the state of single blessedness (the very fact the word "blessedness" is used as description tells much about how they feel toward marriage).

Some of the most gifted men and women through the ages such as Leonardo da Vinci, Samuel Johnson, Vincent van Gogh, Corot, Emily Dickinson, Gertrude Stein, and Amy Lowell, never tried matrimony. They chose to bear out Kipling's adage, "He travels fastest who travels alone."

What are some of the reasons people give for not getting married? The word "freedom" looms large in the arguments of those who choose to remain single. There can be no question that marriage involves the giving up of many liberties precious to the individual, that some freedom will necessarily be sacrificed. These liberties range from such prosaic rights as reading the newspaper while eating breakfast or throwing one's clothes on the bedroom floor, to the more fundamental rights of enjoying long hours of privacy, responsible to no one, or taking a vacation alone and wherever one chooses.

A charming, lively, and intelligent businesswoman of forty recently confided to a friend, "I suppose it would be nice to have the title of 'Mrs.' in front of my name and to have somebody around when I am lonely. But I must admit the older I get, the more I enjoy my freedom. If I were married, could I run off to Europe whenever I please? Could I furnish my apartment exactly to my own taste? Could I sleep as late as I wish on week ends? Could I keep silent when I don't feel like talking? Could I go out with an attractive man if I feel like it? We only live once, so why shouldn't I live the way I find most enjoyable?"

This was no case of sour grapes, because several men had been willing and anxious to marry her. She was quite attached to one man for ten years except for occasional breakups which lasted from two to six months at a time.

Marriage involves responsibilities which many people do not feel they are prepared to assume. Some frankly admit this as did one bachelor of forty-three who asked rhetorically, "Why do I need to take responsibility for a wife and children? What can marriage give me that I don't have now? When I feel the need for feminine company, I lift the telephone and any one of two dozen girls, ranging in age from twenty-one to forty-five, are very happy to go out with me. At the end of the evening I say good-by and don't worry about pleasing anyone. I'm free. I'm enjoying myself. Who needs problems?"

When Careers Come First

Another reason for staying single, once voiced chiefly by men but now increasingly by women also, is the wish to establish oneself in a career. In explaining to a friend why he never married, one surgeon said, "I was graduated from college at twenty-one. I went around with a nice girl whom I liked well enough but we did not have much money and I wanted to go to medical school. If I had married then, it would have meant giving up my career to support a wife. Medical school took another four years and then I was twenty-five.

"Again there was a nice girl, but I knew that before I could support myself, let alone a wife, it would take another few years for me to establish myself. At thirty-five, when I was finally self-supporting, I found I was engaged in a number of vitally important studies and had little time to myself. By now I was accustomed to living alone and liking it. It would have been very difficult for me to break the pattern I had established. I guess I have decided to marry my work."

Women in the theater and movies have publicized the very real dilemma they face in choosing between home and the arduous career of acting. Other women in occupations not so glamorous but just as difficult experience the same conflict. A woman attorney, determined to carve out a career as a specialist in divorce trials, confessed, "I've spent twenty-two years acquiring an education to fit myself for my profession. Why should I throw it away to make some man bacon and eggs every morning and change dirty diapers? I want to be somebody first. For myself alone. Before I become Mrs. Somebody-else."

Because of the increasingly long and expensive preparation for careers, particularly in the professions, it is understandable that some prefer to postpone marriage indefinitely to free themselves for this task of preparation. They have only to look at the married couples around them and see the many sacrifices both partners make if one or both are preparing for a career. If one feels the career is more important than the advantages of marriage, he is probably wiser not to get married, for he would only end up resentful and blaming his partner for standing in the way of success.

Closely related to the problem of establishing oneself in a career, especially for the man, is that of becoming financially independent enough to assume economic responsibility. Many men feel they cannot get married until they are able to support their wives and themselves in a style they feel appropriate to their station in life.

One young bachelor of twenty-eight announced, "I am earning just enough to take care of myself. I live in a decent apartment. I dress fairly well. I can afford the theater whenever I want. Meanwhile, I am working my way up in business. When I reach the point where I have enough money to live comfortably, the way I feel my wife and I should, then I'll be ready to think of marriage."

Ten years later, his salary up to $15,000 a year, he still did not feel he could afford to get married because by then his tastes and expenses had increased even faster than his income. He had been brought up in a home where his father had never been a particularly good provider and his mother often had to take outside employment in addition to raising three children. Very close to his mother in childhood, he sympathized with her in the exhaustion she suffered when after a hard day of work in an office, she had to prepare meals, clean the house, and carry out the many duties of the working mother. Early in life he had vowed never to subject a wife of his to such toil.

The Constant Suitor

Frequently someone who is unmarried will cite his inability to remain faithful to one person, his need for variety in love partners. One man in describing his feelings said, "I know myself well enough not to get married. I meet a girl and fall deeply in love with her. She seems to be all I want in a woman. I court her. I'm not interested in anyone else. For six months it's great. Then just as suddenly as I fell in love, I'm out of it. Maybe I meet someone else who makes her look like Little Orphan Annie. Or maybe I just wake up some morning, open my eyes and say to myself, 'What did I ever see in her?' "

Several of the women who had been involved with this man reported on their experiences with him. One said, "While it lasted, it was sensational. He was attentive, sensitive, tender. He knew how to do all the little things that make a woman feel desirable. Then, all at once, he disappeared and I'd never hear from him again or perhaps get a vague telephone call saying he was busy and would call when he was free."

Another said ruefully, "I bade him farewell at the plane as he flew off for a week end in Chicago and I never saw or heard from him again until a year later when I ran into him on the street."

Apparently some men and women find it impossible to maintain a relationship for any length of time without losing interest or straying to greener fields. They save themselves and their partners much pain if they avoid marriage. The young man described above finally did get married, not once but three times, and each marriage ended in disaster, causing havoc in the lives of the women unfortunate enough to have succeeded in bearing him off to the altar. In one marriage two children were involved, but he also lost interest in them quite quickly.

The mother of this man was a dependent, helpless woman who early in his life succeeded in reversing the customary role of mother and child. In a sense, he mothered her, bringing her breakfast in bed, nursing her through many minor illnesses, listening to her complaints about her husband's inattentiveness, in other words, playing the role of premature parent. One of his deep fears when he became involved with a woman for any length of time was that she, too, would turn into a demanding, dependent woman like his mother who, in a way, had robbed him of a part of normal childhood.

He was unaware of his rage at his mother's refusal to bear the responsibility of caring for him, a rage that was inflicted instead on the many women with whom he became involved in later life and whom he deserted as soon as they showed the slightest sign of leaning on him, a burden he could not accept in the smallest degree. Similarly, his too early assumption of the parental role made it impossible for him to play it properly even when he was chronologically mature enough to do so.

In general, those whose parents have been unable to accept the responsibility of parenthood, and try to thrust it upon their children instead, often have an impaired capacity for a mature relationship later in life. Some may refuse to be drawn into any relationship at all in order to avoid what they experienced as exploitation. In contrast, others repeat the original situation over and over and find themselves mothering many helpless persons, at the same time reacting with considerable anger which they may or may not be aware of, because once again they find themselves in the position of nurturer and get little comfort out of it.

Others seem to come to terms with this problem by developing relationships in which they appear happy to give what they themselves have so sadly lacked. Some find the reparative process which heals the early wound in establishing a mature role for themselves with their children and with a husband or wife.

"There Are No Decent Men"

One oft-mentioned excuse given by the unmarried is the scarcity of suitable mates. It is true that the man or woman who enters the third decade of life unmarried will have some difficulty in finding a fit partner. This problem is more serious for women since our society tends to frown on the woman who marries a younger man, despite the fact that studies show that the chances for happiness in such a marriage are greater than when the partners are the same age or the woman is younger.

A woman of thirty-five is expected to be interested in men of forty or over. An unmarried man that age tends either to have his own reasons for not marrying, such as having to support his parents, or possesses emotional conflicts so acute as to make him a poor risk. However, even men of forty who theoretically have a wide range of possible brides frequently complain of the scarcity of eligible partners. One bachelor of forty-five asked, "Where does one find a truly feminine woman? The few I know are all married. The others are either looking for a meal ticket or are determined to dominate every man they meet. You can't trust most women. You go out with them a few times and as soon as you become involved, they either start demanding things before you're ready to give or run out on you."

This man had been raised in an orphan asylum after his mother died when he was five. At various times he had lived in foster homes where the woman of the house had her own children to whom she showed marked preference. He had grown up suspicious of all women. Fortunately, he finally met a young woman who somehow managed to allay his fears and mistrusts and now at long last is happily married.

In addition to the psychological problems that may cause

the single person to lament the absence of suitable mates, it may well be that the factor of pure chance is operating in that some are not fortunate enough to meet early in life a member of the opposite sex with whom they would be compatible. Some girls very sensibly leave a town in which there is a shortage of eligible males or seek positions where there is greater likelihood of meeting more men. Sometimes the mere improvement of one's chances by a change of environment makes it possible to find and marry a reasonably right man.

An enterprising young woman who worked in a large publishing house where all the editors were married decided to give up her job as copy reader and look for one in a place where some eligible men worked even though it paid less. She selected a large magazine which had a number of bachelors on its staff and within a year was married to a young editor.

"It's a Rotten World"

With nations embroiled in hot and cold wars and the world seemingly drifting toward nuclear disaster, many sensitive men and women raise the objection, "Who wants to get married and bring children into this barbaric era?" A number of them are people with deep social awareness who are appalled by the misery and sorrow they see surging from the four corners of the earth, and who feel they do not want to subject their unborn children to the dangers of an atomic, space-struck age.

Some of the sensitive have probably felt this way since the dawn of history when man first became conscious of the pain and terror life could inflict on him. They believe that perhaps Eve, banished from the Garden of Eden, might better not have brought Cain and Abel into the world.

Problems of the Unmarried

But even when adults have made the choice to remain unmarried for what they believe good and sufficient reasons, they face problems. As they grow older, they are expected to become grouchy and irritable old maids and bachelors, despite the fact that many unmarried older people are very kind, calm, and understanding.

If they are men, their acquaintances are apt to look upon them as gay old dogs living lives of riotous pleasure or as wicked, evil lechers seducing innocent young girls. If they are women they face the social disadvantages of being unmarried and the stigma of having "Miss" before their name.

In this age of intellectualization they are also up against the hazard of the parlor psychoanalyst who, in the course of a casual ten-minute conversation at a party, insists on interpreting the underlying neurotic conflicts which have prevented their being able to marry. Usually the amateur psychoanalyst is both sadistically attacking his helpless victim and using him as a screen on which to project his own neurotic difficulties.

Then there is the question of how to bear the ache of loneliness when everyone else is busy with interests of their own. Closely allied to loneliness is the problem of sexual outlet. Adult men and women who are unmarried still possess the need for sexual expression, although it may not be an urgent one. There is little evidence that frustrating this need by itself leads to serious emotional disorder. It is not true that a sexual outlet is essential for healthy psychic functioning. The point is, rather, that one should be conscious of his sexual feelings, without repressing or denying them, and possess the choice as to whether or not to act on them. As with all else, the extremes are unhappy—either too much repression or too much expression.

For those who are unmarried but who wish to avail themselves of sexual pleasure, organized society places many obstacles in the way. The overwhelming majority of unmarried men manage to override these obstacles, as do an increasingly greater number of women. In the past one outlet available to men was prostitutes and in many areas this is still so. In fact, in two states in the nation prostitution was legal by local option until quite recently, Nevada and Arkansas. But even with glamorous call girls, many men do not find this outlet satisfactory since there is little tenderness or friendship involved.

For women, such an outlet is nonexistent. Stories about male prostitutes available for women whirl out of the wishful thinking of men who imagine this a glorious profession for themselves. One woman, in a letter to the author of a book about call girls, asked, "Why aren't there any Call Men? I am a woman of fifty-two, living with my family in a small town. Sometimes I experience intense desire for a man. I cannot, as do some of the less responsible women in town (I am a high school teacher) go to a bar and pick up a casual companion. If only I could travel to a nearby city and find a Call Man I'd be so much happier."

Another sexual outlet of which a large percentage of those who remain unmarried avail themselves is masturbation. But here the problem may be intensified by the solution. For adults are usually unable to free themselves of childhood feelings of guilt and shame about engaging in this comparatively harmless outlet of self-release even when they understand that enlightened medical opinion no longer believes that masturbation leads either to physical debility or mental deterioration.

A number of those who do not go through the formality of marriage solve the problem by entering into a more or less

permanent relationship without the benefit of legal or cler-
ical sanction. These liaisons may vary from some so permanent as to resemble marriage in everything but name to the
more transitory alliances that last perhaps only a few months.

The satisfaction in such a liaison may be seriously affected
by the community in which the couple live. In some circles,
such as that of the Bohemians who scorn the institutions of
propriety, this is among the most respectable of relationships.
But in a conventional suburban community, such a union
must be carefully guarded or hidden from public view. It is
difficult for most people to enjoy fully a relationship which
they must keep clandestine so as not to be exposed to public
shame.

There are some, on the other hand, who can enjoy a relationship only if it is surrounded by the illicit and the forbidden. One married woman was sexually involved for
sixteen years with a man other than her husband. Finally she
secured a divorce and married her lover. Their marriage
lasted only two months. She found that the love, which had
been so exciting and glamorous when clandestine, became
prosaic when it bore the sanction of church and state.

It is rather rare to find a man who does not marry because
he is tied emotionally to a married woman. Much more common is the case of the unmarried girl who remains in love for
years with a man married to someone else. One young woman
went to work as secretary to a handsome employer when she
was nineteen. Several times during her first year at the office,
it was necessary for them to travel out of town for business
reasons. She found herself more and more attracted to him
and they drifted into sexual intimacy. He was not the mus-
tached villain of melodrama who seduced the poor secretary,
but a perplexed, honest man who found himself genuinely
attracted to a charming young woman as most men would be,

given propinquity and opportunity. At the same time, he
loved his wife and children and refused to break up his home.

Many times he urged his secretary to leave him for an
eligible man and many times she tried going out with other
men. But inevitably she found herself comparing the other
men unfavorably to her married lover and finally she decided
she would rather spend one night a week with him, sharing
him with his wife, than spend all her time with a husband
who bored her. She has settled for this way of life for the
last twenty years and somehow seems to have made peace
within herself.

Others do not get involved in a permanent liaison either
with a married or unmarried partner but attempt to keep
their sexual lives at a very casual level by indulging in a
series of brief affairs with little or no emotional involvement.
Here, too, the woman finds such a solution much more difficult than does the man. As one woman put it, "I can't enjoy
sex without love. If I go to bed with a man, I feel I love
him. If I don't love him, I won't have sex with him. Maybe
men can have just sex and get away with it, but when I tried,
it was too painful and I gave it up."

This seems to be the feeling of most women. Here the emotional difference between the sexes makes itself evident, for
despite all efforts at sexual equality men and women are
quite different, so that while many men apparently do enjoy
casual sexual encounters, very few women are able to do so
without suffering shame and guilt. Most women seem to have
to feel "in love with" a man before they can give themselves
sexually.

Those Who Wish To Marry but Cannot

If, after considering all the reasons why it may not be wise
to marry or even too important whether one marries, a man

or woman still feels anxious to get married, it might be worthwhile to examine some of the conflicts that stand in the way of those who like the idea of marriage but find it difficult to accept a specific mate.

One of the characteristics that keeps people from getting married goes by the technical name of "narcissism." It is a quality that everyone possesses as a child, but as one grows older, a certain amount of narcissism is given up and instead there develops an interest toward and concern for others. We all retain some of our narcissism—again, it is a matter of degree.

Some cannot give up enough of their narcissism to enjoy anyone else. We have all experienced the overt narcissist, the person who, in a restaurant, instead of conversing with his dinner partner is engaged in a tempestuous love affair with himself, busy affectionately patting his hair, casting long, admiring glances at his reflection in the mirror or looking around constantly to see if anyone is watching him. This kind of self-involvement makes any relationship, especially the one that is probably the most complicated and demanding of all, marriage, extremely difficult if not impossible.

The opposite side of the coin of self-centeredness is shown by the one who is constantly concerned with his own shortcomings. There are those who, instead of self-admiration, consider it the height of fascinating conversation to regale everyone with a long list of their failings. The "poor little me" attitude signifies just as intense a preoccupation with the "me" as the self-admirer.

Another sign of self-concern has sprung into existence because of new psychological knowledge, misused in this instance. One young lady spent most of her time on a date giving her escort a complete run-down on the latest state of her personality. Every complex, suppression, and inhibition, not to mention defense, rationalization, and projection, was unflinchingly exposed to the awareness of the listener, and she had great difficulty understanding why, when she was willing to give so much of herself, most men did not want any part of her.

This type of mental hypochondriac has, in the more sophisticated circles, replaced the old-fashioned hypochondriac who is sadly limited to description of physical aches and pains, such as vagaries of the digestive system or heart. Both the physical and psychological hypochondriac are equally preoccupied with the self.

Another type of narcissism is shown by the person who says he feels "self-conscious" and who is literally describing the cause of his unhappiness. It would become even clearer if he reversed the order of the two words and inserted three additional ones—"conscious only of the self."

All three, the self-conscious person and the physical, as well as the psychological hypochondriac, would benefit by developing a lively curiosity about the people around them instead of limiting their interest to their own problems. Some, unfortunately, possess conflicts so deep it is impossible for them to divert much of their attention to others.

One young woman who is strikingly beautiful avoids discussing her physical aches but devotes her conversation almost exclusively to a description of the many vicissitudes she suffers on the job and in her personal life. Everyone she meets immediately becomes her confidante and she pours into their often unwilling ears a stream of intimate details about the latest outrages committed upon her by employer, co-worker, parent, and lover. Should the conversation shift to any other subject, she withdraws and sits back, ostensibly an idyllic picture of intense contemplation. When asked about what she is thinking at such moments, she promptly resumes her dramatic narrative of the trials and tribulations she is currently combating.

Another characteristic of the self-centered person is his search for someone to fill a need for love that is insatiable. He may describe the need as admiration, support, praise, warmth, friendship, or love, but always it is in terms of *his* need. All too often, every relationship turns to ashes on the altar of his burning hunger. Such unhappy people are most often the product of three kinds of upbringing, either neglect, overindulgence, or the frequent swing between these two states, all designed to create an individual with needs so powerful as to cause any prudent partner to beat a rapid retreat to someone more easily satisfied.

Essentially this insatiability is a wish to duplicate the early stages of life when all needs were fulfilled by the ever-present mother. With maturity, we learn to renounce the insatiability in part and bear the frustration of not having all our wishes granted at the moment we make the demands. As we are able to do this, we can think of another's needs in addition to our own. It is enlightened self-interest to make oneself sensitive to other people because most successful relationships are based on the meeting of each other's needs. If each one screams "me first, me first," there is apt to be little give and take between two people.

Another vital problem that faces some who cannot marry is fear of their sexual feelings, a fear that may be expressed in many ways. One woman, a competent, successful personnel executive with a major corporation, in her dealings with superiors, co-workers, and others whom she encounters in the business world, is a model of cool, smooth efficiency. Reasonably attractive, trim and well-groomed, she is often invited by men to dinner or the theater. Suddenly, although able to handle the myriad details of her work with little apparent difficulty, she feels like an inarticulate, perspiring schoolgirl on her first date. So painful does she find these social occasions, that often she lets months go by during which she prefers the loneliness of her small apartment to the terror of a date.

She is an extreme example of the fear that some of the unmarried feel toward members of the opposite sex. In many instances the fears are more difficult to fathom, not as obvious as in her case. Another woman who claims she enjoys going out with men is often attacked by searing headaches and nausea on the day of an important date. A third woman finds herself the victim of the twenty-four-hour virus when she is slated for a date. One man becomes overwhelmed by the sudden realization that his work has piled up when he is supposed to squire a young lady around town for an evening's entertainment. All these suffer from fear of the opposite sex. Sometimes they fear that their intense feelings of either love or hate may get out of control in a close relationship. Sometimes they fear arousing in the other person feelings of love or hate, not knowing how to deal with them.

One woman became emotionally involved with a man she saw only during business hours. For two years she made no effort to change their relationship into a more personal one, waiting with increasing desperation for him to take the first step. Meanwhile she discouraged every other man, believing herself in love with this one, puzzled because he would make no effort to become better friends. Finally she confided her feelings to a mutual friend who looked at her in wonder and said, "Don't you know this is a man very much afraid of being loved? He recognizes in your warm femininity a capacity for emotions of a depth that frighten him. He prefers to avoid any entanglement."

This woman realized she had been attracted to a series of

such men who would find her pleasant and charming as long as the contacts remained superficial but who would walk away as soon as the feelings showed any signs of deepening. She also realized that her father, to whom she had been very much attached, had always been cool and detached, and that with these men she was re-enacting the hopeless little drama of her youth, trying to arouse the remote man who was like her father.

One handsome young man, a scion of a socially prominent family, had serious difficulties with drinking. After several years of imbibing to the point where he was concerned about the danger of becoming an alcoholic, he decided to give up liquor. Two years after his decision, during which time he had not touched a drop of alcohol, he met an old girl friend he had known at college where he had been very much attracted to her but too shy to court her. In the ensuing eight years she had been married and divorced and become the mistress of one of the country's leading financiers, her escapades described in the society and gossip columns of some of the more sensational newspapers, all of which only increased the young man's interest in her. To his surprise, she greeted him warmly and was quite receptive to his invitation to supper the following week.

The next day he started to drink. Startled by his sudden slip from the wagon, he examined the reasons for his behavior. With the aid of the therapist who had helped him understand the reasons for his alcoholism, he realized he needed the bottled courage because of the fear as to how well he would perform sexually with a young lady of such sophistication. He had been married for five years to a woman who would lecture him after practically every sexual intimacy on his many shortcomings in the amorous arts.

Despite two subsequent affairs in which he acquitted himself to the apparent satisfaction of his partners, the five years of wifely brainwashing had reinforced his own sense of inadequacy, since he had always suffered from a pervasive fear and anxiety about all of his aptitudes, amorous and otherwise. His early life had been spent with a severely critical mother and sisters, so that the wife's derogation fell on fertile ground. His fear sprouted into the full bloom of sexual panic when he faced what he regarded as the test of his masculinity.

Fear of Sexual Pleasure

Despite increasing education about sex, many men and women are still beset with a fear so powerful that not only does it interfere with the functioning of mature sexuality, but it actually prevents romantic involvements with the opposite sex. Some women, the unaware victims of sexual fear, deliberately keep themselves unattractive so no man will become interested enough to expose them to the danger of intimacy.

One such woman maintained her protection from temptation through overweight. She reached for a sweet instead of the sweetness of romance. Then she fell ill and lost fifty pounds. Before she could eat herself back to safety she met a man who fell in love with her and asked her to marry him. Without the buttress of excess poundage she was vulnerable, and escaped into a nervous breakdown rather than face the perils of relating to a man.

Some men who rail against the faults of the women they encounter, concentrating with deep satisfaction on all the flaws they observe in the feminine inhabitants of the world, are disguising their fear in these attacks.

Sexual fear is founded on a number of things, one of them being the early repeated prohibitions against touching one's own body. Overt, spoken prohibitions, however, are not the only means of making a child afraid of his sexuality. Unspoken attitudes, not only of parents but of a society that frowns on sexual pleasure, helps load the natural instinct with an overlay of fear.

The child discovers the genital area of his body during his infantile exploratory movements, and he also discovers it is pleasurable to stimulate these areas himself or rub himself up against adults when possible. Even the most well-meaning parents, because of their own early experiences, find it difficult not to react to natural, childish sexual activity with fear, disgust, or punitiveness. Some enlightened parents may control any conscious expression of their fear or refrain from punishing the child but will still unconsciously convey to the child that genital pleasure is wrong and dirty, perhaps by pulling his hand away or attempting to divert his attention.

An extreme measure to prevent a young boy's masturbating at night in his sleep was taken by one mother and father who hired a nurse to sit and watch while he slept and remove his hand when he started to masturbate. Usually parents are not this concerned, knowing that after a while the child will give up masturbation, usually when he becomes active in schoolwork and athletics.

Since much of the prohibition against genital pleasure is enforced even before the child knows words, genital pleasure is apt to be experienced in later life with a dread that is literally "nameless." It is for this reason that many individuals who consciously accept the desirability of sexual pleasure still find themselves encompassed by a fear that stems from the wordless days of infancy, a fear they seem unable to assuage.

Sexual fear is intensified by the prohibition, continued over the years of growing up, against most sensual pleasure and particularly against sexual pleasure. The Puritan influence on our culture is by no means dissipated, so that many of us as adults are still nagged by feelings of guilt about our wishes for pleasure. We may even feel it wicked, for instance, to enjoy ourselves too much except on a regular vacation when one is supposed to have fun. Sexual pleasure is usually forbidden most emphatically to females, for parents, no matter how enlightened, differentiate in urging much greater restraint for girls than boys.

Sexual prohibitions apply first within the family where erotic arousal necessarily starts, since the members of one's family are the first human beings one knows and over the early years remain the closest. Some parents will heedlessly permit brothers and sisters to bathe together, a very unwise procedure because it may cause erotic stimulation the child is unable to handle. In contrast, other parents go to fantastic lengths to prevent even the simplest and most natural contacts between brothers and sisters, such as hugging or kissing.

Even more powerful than the prohibition of erotic play between brothers and sisters is that against the expression of such feelings between parent and child. While this prohibition is necessary, sometimes the way in which a parent enforces it may affect the child's future emotional feelings. The little boy who wishes to climb into bed and snuggle close to his mother and who is sternly ordered out of the bed by a father who treats him as though he were committing a crime (out of the father's own fear of competition and possibly a fear, too, of his own sexual feelings) may feel this rebuke caused by his wish for feminine warmth. Such early prohibitions may pervade his later life, so that the young boy ordered harshly out of bed and away from his mother, now growing to manhood, has operating within his head the unconscious command, "Stay away from a woman. She is taboo."

Not only may fear of sex in an adult result from severe prohibition but it may also result from too much sexual stimulation as a child. Some parents act overseductively with children. One divorced mother customarily went to her son's bedroom every night, clad in the filmiest of negligees, to lean over and tenderly kiss him good night on the lips. Recalling this in later years, he was filled with fury at his mother for arousing in him erotic feelings which it was impossible for him to handle and which caused him many sleepless hours, as well as fear-provoking guilt.

As a man, the rage he felt at his mother's seductive behavior and his consequent fury and guilt was transferred to other women, particularly those who acted seductively toward him. Such men find it impossible very often to become close to warm, friendly women but choose the detached type who live in their own cloud world, so that seductive behavior, or any behavior that could possibly be interpreted as seductive, does not act as a barrier by raising their old fear.

Prohibitions, within limits are needed for children, for incest cannot be sanctioned. The temperate, middle-of-the-path approach is the happy one between parent and child. The child must learn tenderness and affection but he must not be seduced out of his wits by being hungrily over-hugged, over-kissed and over-petted because of the parent's own uncontrolled sexual needs. Nor should there be the unpredictable shifts, as there are in some families, between ardent affection one moment and strong rejection the next.

The Dream of the Perfect Lover

Many of the unwillingly unmarried find themselves alone in the world for a reason only too well known. They expect too much. These are the unhappy men and women who have lived for years with their fantasies of the perfect mate and insist that reality provide them with a counterpart of their dream lover.

Highly imaginative, they are capable of constructing in their mind individuals so magnificent that even the most perfect of men or women would be so far beneath the imaginary lover that it is impossible for them to compromise with their dream. They usually do not put it in such terms, even to themselves, but instead concentrate on the very real weaknesses they find in the people they meet in everyday life, forgetting that the truly flawless person, if such a freak were to exist, would be the most boring of partners.

Sometimes the creation of idealized fantasy mates is a result of early loneliness when the child peopled his imaginary world with wonderful playmates to make up for the lack of real friends. For the imaginatively gifted, these colorful fantasy products may seem so satisfactory in later life that it is difficult to give them up in favor of the comparative grayness that reality offers.

As one young man put it, after years of struggle that finally ended in a successful break with the world of fantasy, and attachment to the world of reality, "It was sick and destructive to myself to live in my world of grand opera. All the people I associated with in my head were splendid heroes and heroines, not like the mundane, boring characters surrounding me, but I had no way of knowing then that I had created them because of the pain of reality."

He gradually became content with the more real if less colorful individuals with whom he was now able to relate. He found part of his opera of the mind in reality by marrying a rather uninhibited young lady, capable of flights of dramatic love-making as well as occasional flights of dramatic brawling. He confessed he enjoyed the intense awareness of these highly charged encounters more than the most extravagant creations of his imagination.

Another man, a successful scientist in his late thirties, is respected for his achievements, including the publication of a number of papers in eminent scientific journals describing intricate, precise experiments which he has carried to fruition. But he has been unable to establish any sort of liaison with a woman that lasts beyond three or four dates.

He is often attracted to young women who find him interesting and engaging and make it quite clear they would welcome his serious attentions. Sooner or later, though, he breaks off the relationship with extreme revulsion, usually commenting, in words so similar as to show the existence of a rather rigid pattern, "I thought she was lovely when I first met her but she turned out to be a slob. A pig. Just like all the others. The way she stuffed food into her mouth, the way she sloshed coffee in her cup, revolted me. I couldn't get away from her soon enough."

If it was not the food, it was the careless way she dressed, or the untidiness of her apartment, or the too-lavish make-up she wore. Always it was a reaction against what he considered sloppiness, filth, dirt, and disorder—the imperfections of manners and body.

He had been raised by a mother who was known throughout the community for the sparkling, tidy cleanliness of her home. She maintained this cleanliness both by working very hard to achieve it and by insisting that her husband and children be extremely neat around the house. At the age of six, her son was responsible for cleaning his own room and he had to take off his dirty shoes before entering the house each day so as not to track up the spotless kitchen (no member of the family was permitted to enter the home except through the rear door).

Instead of rebelling against this excessive show of cleanliness, as many children in similar circumstances have done, for it is a child's nature not to be neat, to want everything cleaned up for him if clean he must be, this boy accepted all his mother's strictures and, if anything, attempted to improve on them. In his chosen profession of science, this compulsive orderliness was very much of an asset and made his experimental procedures a model of precision. Unfortunately, he looked for similar order and precision in his personal relations where he was unable to find it since human beings do not exist as though they were meant to live in sterile laboratories.

Fear of Childbirth

Sometimes a reluctance to marry can be traced to a fear not so much of marriage but the consequence of marriage, children. Women who have been raised on old wives' tales about the pain of childbirth may be afraid of experiencing excruciating distress, if not actually of dying. Frequently these tales were not imparted directly but the fear stemmed from overhearing older women boasting competitively of the torture they endured when they gave birth. To the young girl not yet able to distinguish between truth and dramatic embellishment, hearing such stories can be a terror-inspiring experience, so that at the thought of marriage the terror is revived and directed against not just the possibility of having children but the whole concept of marriage.

One woman of forty knew she felt a deep fear of having children but never knew why until one day, in discussing it with a friend, she recalled that her own mother had endured great pain in giving birth to her and had nearly died. Over the years she had felt guilt at causing her mother such agony and unconsciously had determined not to go through such pain herself. It is a fact that those women whose own mothers have had a fairly easy time of childbirth are the ones who do not fear it and thus experience less pain as they give birth.

Men too may be affected by this fear but in a different way of course, their fear focusing on the pain they may cause a loved one. Since a popular accompanying lament to the tale of the misery of childbearing goes, "If only men knew what we suffered," young boys who hear this may decide they will never subject a woman they love to such suffering. The surest guarantee against causing or enduring the pain of childbirth is to stay away from marriage and the possibilities of pregnancy.

Another fear shared by both men and women is that of producing a monstrous or deformed child. Though this rarely occurs, the possibility of spawning a defective human being does haunt some people and may be so intense as to prevent them from ever becoming expectant parents.

One cause of the fear of producing a monster is the feeling that one is, in some respect, monstrous himself. This is only one of the many kinds of feelings of unworthiness with which people plague themselves, for a recurrent fear in many of the unmarried is that they are not worthy of marriage.

Fear of Unworthiness

They may believe this feeling is a result of not having attracted a worthwhile mate, but more likely it is just the opposite—the difficulty in attracting a mate is caused by the conviction of their own unworthiness. If one feels unworthy, physically or mentally, monstrous or deficient in some respect, one may hope to hide it from superficial acquaintances but one can hold little hope of concealing it from such an intimate acquaintance as husband or wife is apt to be. In order to avoid the intimacy which will lead to exposure of what they feel as their unworthiness, there are those who will not risk a closeness that could lead to marriage.

Some who suffer for years because of feelings of inferiority and fear of exposure will sometimes brave this fear, bare their feelings to one they love and find, to their astonishment, that the other is not disgusted or shocked. The longer one waits to make this revelation the more difficult it becomes, but it is rarely impossible if one feels secure enough with someone and realizes that we all, at times, have feelings of unworthiness that are not real.

Some fear their unworthiness is discoverable only by members of the opposite sex and may feel more comfortable in spending most of their time with members of their own sex. To them the threat of rejection seems confined to rejection by the opposite sex. One vivacious nurse, Helen, in her early thirties, was the dynamic center of a group of young career women. She frequently was invited to affairs which were usually in the nature of group parties in that several young men would invite several young women over for drinks, or vice versa. At several of these parties she aroused the interest of a young man who asked if he could take her home, but each time she explained she had come with her friends and did not think it proper to leave without them.

One evening, when one of her friends broke the unspoken compact among the women and allowed a man to take her home, Helen was furious at this "betrayal." When the rebel compounded her traitorship by marrying the man, Helen started to face her feelings and see that her fury had been colored by envy. She then announced that next time a man asked to escort her home, she would accept. She realized she had been using her friendship with the women as a defensive alliance to protect herself against the fear of the enemy—man.

Men, too, may band together in mutual defense tactics as they glowingly describe how much fun they have when they go "out with the boys," playing poker or bridge, shooting pool, hunting or fishing or golfing, or making the rounds of bars in exclusively masculine company. We all have a need for friends of the same sex with whom we spend a reasonable amount of time, and the wise woman accepts a man's need for masculine friends. Rather than offering objection, she encourages him to see friends of his own with whom he can spend time away from her. She also reserves for herself the same right for feminine friendships.

This granting of greater freedom and flexibility to each other often fosters a better relationship between a couple, married or unmarried, because it prevents each from feeling constrained by the exclusive possessiveness of the other and it provides outside experiences which each can then bring back to the other and share. If one feels insecure with a mate or fiancé, so that his every acquaintance, regardless of the sex, is looked upon as a threat, it is difficult to permit such freedom and the relationship has to endure one more strain.

Too Tight a Tie to Parents

Last, but far from least, of the ties that prevent permanent binding to a mate, is the attachment of the unmarried adult to his parent. Some of these attachments are based on real and pressing circumstances. The lonely, widowed mother who has only the loyal child to support her, financially and psychologically, offers a conflict that makes it morally difficult for the child to leave and start a family of his own.

Sometimes, though, the dependence of the parent may be primarily a product of the son's or daughter's own wish to be needed. A fairly successful businessman in his early forties has made a comfortable home for himself and his mother in a middle-class suburb ever since his discharge from the Army after World War II. Albert is a good dancer, dresses well, and is much in demand for social occasions when a spare man is needed.

Many of his married friends indulge in matchmaking forays in an effort to get him married. At times the matchmaking appears to take, for Albert and the woman begin to see each other with some regularity and he finds he enjoys her company. Then the inevitable occurs as the woman starts to drop hints about marriage and the matchmakers question Albert about his intentions. At such times he invariably replies, "She is a lovely woman and I would be proud to have her for a wife. But I don't see how I could do this to Mom. My sister and brother are busy with their own families and Mom would be lonely if I didn't spend most of my time with her. I'm all she has. Now don't get me wrong. Mom would love to see me married. In fact, she's always asking me when I'm going to get married and wants me to bring my lady friends around to meet her. But I feel I can't do that to her."

Discouraged by the firmness of his resolution not to abandon "Mom," the young women usually break away reluctantly. Albert is again left to serve as the extra man at a party and be a challenge to someone else's vain matchmaking proclivities.

A woman of thirty-five named Frances, whose father died when she was twenty-one and her younger sister Charlotte was eighteen, continued to live at home with her mother and sister. She went to work to earn money to put her sister through college. As she explained, "Charlotte was always my parents' favorite. I knew both my father and mother wanted her to have a college education so I pitched in and helped her get one."

As soon as Charlotte was graduated, she married, leaving Frances to live alone with her mother. Frances went out with men occasionally but always insisted they bring her home early so her mother would not be alone. Increasingly, she found her relationship with her mother more satisfactory than with anyone else.

"We're not like mother and daughter, not even like sisters —we're more like very close friends," she told a friend enthusiastically. "She understands me and I understand her. Sometimes we don't even need words. Why, the other day I went into the bedroom while my mother was in the living room, and I started to hunt for my stockings. My mother called out from the living room, 'They're in the second drawer.' I didn't have to say a word and she knew what I wanted."

It is remarkable how often the less favored child sacrifices himself to remain the loyal protector of the bereaved parent. Shakespeare described this situation with his customary poetic insight in King Lear when the deprived youngest daughter became the one who elected to remain with the aged king and protect him after he had ignored her and left his fortune to the two older daughters.

This effort is generally an attempt of the child who feels himself less loved to attain the love he finds lacking. Sometimes, because they are so anxious to obtain love, children may overlook a parent's capacity to fend for himself. One man, who finally succeeded in breaking the silver cord and marrying, described with great surprise how much better his mother was doing now that he was out of the house. Whereas formerly she had centered her whole life around him, she was now finding friends and companions her own age and was obviously much happier than in the former restricted relationship.

There are parents who act quite tyrannical in their wish to hold onto a daughter or son who should long since have tried his psychic wings. But if this desire does not arouse an answering response in the child, based on his own dependent needs, it is not very effective and can be combated by a son or daughter who truly wishes to get married, who does not believe that if a mother or father must live alone it will necessarily mean they will perish from want of attention.

Sometimes bondage to the parent is not expressed as concretely as actually living together, but may exist chiefly on an emotional level, so that even though thousands of miles separate son or daughter from father or mother, the child still remains loyal to the parental image. He does not wish to be untrue to his parent, even though he may not see the parent for months or years. The parent may even be dead and the image still linger on in the child's mind, as strong as ever. Such people do not realize the truest loyalty one can show to a parent is to become a parent oneself. Imitation in procreation is the sincerest form of flattery.

Those who are unmarried and who have decided this is the state in which they wish to remain should have the courage of their convictions and not yield to the pressures of conformity by marrying against their better judgment, because a marriage entered into for such a reason will most certainly fail.

Those who are willing but seem unable to marry might study themselves to see whether this inability is based on factors beyond their control, in which case they may find other compensations to enrich their lives. But if the causes for inability to marry lie within themselves, they can seek to change, if they wish, by facing their conflicts and taking whatever steps, including psychiatric help, may be needed.

It is amazing how many men and women wait until the comparatively advanced years of their forties and fifties to first enter into marriages which are sometimes more successful than the unions of impetuous youth.

13 THE ONCE MARRIED, NOW LONELY

Somehow the experience of having been married, even for a very short time, seems to leave an indelible mark on those who have undertaken it. Men and women who were once married but no longer live with their mates because of separation, divorce, or death, face problems similar to the unmarried, though frequently of a special intensity, as well as problems unique to them.

Separation is the most ambiguous state. Those who are neither divorced nor widowed but live apart from their mates, while yet tied in tenuous manner, probably have the most difficult and complicated of times in finding new partners.

The separated fall into two classes, as a rule. There are, first, those who think of the separation as temporary while they go their own way for awhile and try to think things through. Perhaps they have quarreled so seriously that they feel it impossible to live with each other until the wounds have healed, or perhaps one or the other has been deeply hurt and wants time by himself to recover.

Then there is the second class of separatees who are, for all intents and purposes except the legal one, as good as divorced. This group includes those who cannot afford the financial cost of a formal divorce, those who for religious reasons do not believe in divorce but have no intention of ever again living with each other, and those who have just never gone to the trouble of getting a divorce because they have not wished to marry anyone else. Strangely enough, the latter comprise a surprisingly large number of men and women.

The so-called "temporary separation" is, for many, probably the closest one can come to limbo while still in the land of the living. It is a state of suspended animation in which one feels not truly alive nor truly dead, neither in heaven nor hell but in some mid-point of dead calm. So intolerable is this state for some people that, although they may have been functioning fairly well in a miserable marriage, they find themselves paralyzed, unable to adjust to any aspect of life when they first separate. This is related to the agony of being torn away from someone who has been close, even though now he may be experienced as a hateful human being.

The state of indecision that characterizes many separations is another difficulty to be endured, as one woman found out. After an engagement that lasted ten years, Bettina finally married the man to whom for so long she had been betrothed. During her lengthy engagement, whose culmination in marriage was prevented by many real obstacles, including her fiancé's four-year service in the Army, her mother's severe illness, and then her fiancé's effort to establish himself financially so as to be able to afford marriage, Bettina yearned constantly for the security of marriage. But, once married, she found to her distress that instead of affording the answer to her problems, marriage hatched a new flock of conflicts.

Her husband, with whose needs she became somewhat

familiar during the engagement, turned into a far more demanding man. He insisted on supervising how she dressed, the way she cooked, and the care of their house. In addition, he required constant reassurance and, since Bettina was not a very articulate woman, it was difficult for her to express her approval and admiration of his prowess as often as he wished it.

At the end of three years they went away for a long summer vacation and, for once, the marriage seemed to be going well. He made fewer demands and she found it easier to express the real admiration she felt for many of his qualities, even though she still believed he asked too much of her.

As she was packing for the return journey, she picked up an old jacket of her husband's. A small package of letters fell out of one of the pockets. Idly she looked at the top one. She was frozen into immobility as she realized that her husband was having an affair with some young girl. Even as Bettina had thought things were going so much better in her marriage, her husband had been telephoning his mistress long distance.

When the outraged wife confronted her husband with the evidence and demanded that he end the affair at once or she would leave him, he flatly refused to make any promises even though he was disenchanted with his extramarital situation himself (and possibly had unconsciously left the letters where they would be found). He resented his wife's dictatorial attitude and they separated.

Not long afterward the husband turned into an ardent wooer, making every effort to win his wife back. But a strange thing was happening to her. She had never been free before, since she had moved directly from her mother's home into marriage. She discovered that living alone offered many compensations. Yet she was torn, for she frequently felt pangs of loneliness as she sat alone in her furnished room at night. More devastating than the loneliness, and overshadowing the pleasures of freedom, however, was the ambiguity of her position. What should she do next? Would she be able to go out with other men? While she suspected that her husband was still seeing the other woman, she felt she should not accept the attentions of other men while she was legally married.

It was her doubt, her inability to decide what to do, that she found most trying during this period. Sometimes she felt that to take either path, divorce from a man for whom she still felt some love, or return to a man she still hated for his betrayal of her, was preferable to this suspended way of life. She realized that until she was able either to give up her husband or to forgive him, it would be impossible for her to make or help him make a satisfactory decision.

The Paralysis of Indecision

One of the requirements for ending the suspense of a temporary separation is to decide what action to take. Often indecision is due not only to the ambiguity of the state of separation but the ambiguity of feelings—does the person want to return to his mate or give him up permanently?

For some, the separation may serve as a sort of breather before making the next move, either a return to the marriage to try to work it out or on to divorce. For others, the separation comes as a blessed relief from the pressures of a tormenting, tempestuous marriage that somehow must be ended before it results in mutual destruction.

Sometimes just getting away from a desperate situation enables one to reach a decision which would have been impossible had he remained in it. Only as he can escape the whirlpool of marital fury is he able to understand more of his own part in creating crises and the purpose such deadly drama has been serving in his own life.

One wife seemed unable to break up a marriage that at

times seemed more horrible than any nightmare. In our night-mares we never die, but she felt her husband might actually kill her in a moment of drunken rage as he sometimes threatened to do. They were both sensitive and intellectual, he being a teacher of literature in high school and she a commercial artist and, not understanding the anger that burst forth from him, she kept making excuses for it.

He would drink excessively, then accuse her of not living up to her promise as a wife, sometimes striking her in fury and calling her foul names. One day, after a particularly vicious attack during which he kept her up all night, she decided to leave in spite of the fact that she knew that both she and her husband dreaded giving up the marriage and confessing to their friends they had failed. She felt confused as to what to do, since she had given up a good job to marry him, left her home in a distant city, and she knew practically no one in the city where they now lived. But she decided that to live as she had been doing, with a man possessed by a fury she never dreamed existed, was too degrading to bear any longer.

She moved to a hotel and they lived apart for two months. She used her savings to support herself for he gave her not a penny. He kept calling her up at all hours of the day and night, begging her to return, promising he would not lose his temper any more and assuring her they could make a go of it if they would only try harder. At first she refused to return, then out of loneliness and moved by a remnant of former love, she moved back to their apartment.

For a month it was idyllic, then once again he started to shout at her and get drunk and slap her, and once again she went through the conflict of whether to stay. It took her another few months, during which time he made no attempt to have sexual intimacy, before she realized this was a marriage that would never work. There was too much fear and anger between them. Their choice of each other was founded on such fantasy that it was impossible for either to fulfill the other's demands.

When she told him she was going to get a divorce, he refused to accept her decision. "You don't dare leave me," he sneered. "You'll have nothing. You couldn't stand it once and you won't be able to now."

It took courage but she returned to her home city and her former job. The first separation had given her a sense of the futility of the marriage, but she had determined to try once more, knowing it would not succeed. She realized that what was wrong with their relationship would never right itself unless both of them received psychological help, he for his drunkenness, she for her need to marry a man who would inflict physical and psychological cruelty upon her, and her inability to leave when his basic brutality became clear to her, for she had, in all, lived with him almost two years.

Unfortunately, for some people there is little guarantee that the passage of time alone will improve the ability to divine their true feelings, and the struggle to arrive at a purity of feeling may well be a hopeless one. Most of us learn that generally we have to settle for the stronger of two contradictory feelings rather than achieving monolithic unity. It is not always necessary to choose between love and hate, and in most of our relations with people we feel a little of both and do not usually expect to possess a feeling undiluted by its opposite. The ability to tolerate this mixture of feeling is one of the criteria of emotional maturity.

In the case of the wife mentioned above, there was so much open anger on the part of her husband and so great a need on her part to be beaten by him physically and psychologically that there was no chance for love to fight its way through the violence. Here was no mixture of love and hate, but rather an overabundance of hatred.

Sometimes the problem is not in knowing how one feels—for one may know his feelings only too well—but the difficulty may lie in knowing how to act on the feelings. One wife, separated from her husband, realized she loved him and wanted him back, but she felt she could not make the first move. Some women stay separated because "pride" prevents them from lifting the receiver and making a simple telephone call.

The Proud Are Often Lonely

One of the psychological monsters we create within ourselves which robs us of opportunities for happiness is false pride. Many men and women have lived out a life of loneliness trying to comfort themselves with the futile thought, "At least I have my pride." If pride is that important, it will be difficult to establish a close relationship with anyone, for in living with someone we occasionally have to sacrifice pride in the interests of harmony.

The word "pride" as defined by Webster has two almost contradictory meanings. One definition is "a sense of one's own dignity or worth," "self-respect," while the other more accepted meaning of the word is "an overhigh opinion of oneself," "exaggerated self-esteem," "conceit." Actually the second definition is the opposite of the first. The person who possesses a true sense of his own dignity finds no need for exaggerated self-esteem which usually hides a lack of feeling of worth. The person aware of his own worth need have no fear about compromising it by making a telephone call to ask someone he loves to return, or to ask if he may return to someone he loves. The great personages of this world have not been known for their pride. The Bible says "Pride goeth before destruction" and this is particularly true in marriage where the inordinate pride of one or both often "goeth be-fore" the destruction of the marriage.

It sometimes happens that the insistent demands of one partner that the other return defeats its own purpose, for the demand is not based on love but on getting one's own way. It is helpful, if one mate truly wishes the other back, for both to sit down and rationally decide what would best achieve the healing of the marital fracture. One remedy is to remem-ber what has helped or hindered in previous quarrels.

A wife, whose husband had left her, used their first subse-quent meetings as opportunities to express her resentment and remind him of how poor a husband he had been. Yet each time he left, she felt utterly miserable and wondered how she could manage to bring about a reconciliation. Finally, she discussed the situation with a wise friend who recommended that she try a change of approach.

At the next meeting she was warm, friendly, and close, as she had been during the first days of their marriage, instead of being abusive and critical. Her husband eagerly accepted the new attitude, made ardent love to her, and at the end of the evening she told him how happy she had been with him.

Without saying a word, the next day the husband moved back. Now, fifteen years later, with two children in school, this wife has never forgotten the wisdom of substituting ac-ceptance for criticism.

Some persons, particularly men, find temporary separation, as it becomes of almost permanent duration, a secure hideout against deep emotional entanglements with anyone new. They feel free to woo many women and marry none, always having the perfect answer to the feminine wish for marriage by claim-ing exemption because of their already-married state. They cling to a relationship that has failed, not daring to attempt a new one because of their fear of another failure.

This is a far from satisfying way of living, for it does not solve the problem of aloneness. It seems impossible to banish loneliness by indulging in a series of transitory, superficial affairs. Sometimes these even heighten a sense of loneliness, as the inevitable ending in which one is either abandoned or abandons, revives over and over the anguish of emptiness.

No matter how unpleasant they may have found their marriage, most of those who get divorced and do not immediately remarry seem to go through a period of mourning in which they find themselves adrift for the lack of customary moorings. Marriage with its routine and regularities does give some feeling of stability and when one is suddenly uprooted from it, he usually experiences a sense of loss. Then comes a time of readjustment when, once again, the person has to learn to live by himself. It is not easy to resume social life, for most of the friends that couples make are mutual and there is often a sense of strain at attempting to continue a friendship founded on another basis. No matter how much friends try to remain neutral, they are apt to feel more loyalty toward one than the other.

The Not-So-Gay Divorcée

Divorced women also face the problem of being frequently a special target for every predatory male. The idea of "gay divorcée," usually more true in fiction than fact, seems to pervade the minds of many men. Women who have been married are likely to be more interested in continuing sexual experience than those who have never been married, and statistics show that the divorced woman or man has a better chance of marrying again than the one who has never married.

The most serious problem divorcées face is to guard against duplicating the first marriage. All too often, the divorced, although aware of the difficulties encountered with their recently discarded spouse, leap from marital frying pan into marital fire by marrying someone who is similar in many ways, not only psychologically but physically, to the mate from whom they have moved away.

It is therefore important that before they remarry, they examine closely whether they are not committing the same error once again. Second marriages often work out better than the first but usually both partners have profited from their past experiences and are determined not to make the same mistakes twice.

Excessive doubt and endless analysis may make it difficult ever to remarry, but if one uses the period of readjustment after the divorce to face honestly his own difficulties which may have contributed, first to the choice of an unsuitable mate, and second, to the conflicts that arose within the marriage, he is likely to be in a much better position to make an intelligent second choice.

The Bonds of Alimony

One special problem that sometimes prevents women from remarrying is the institution of alimony. While a woman who is left with children has every right to expect her husband to contribute to their support, this is very different from the exorbitant demands for alimony made by many women, often spurred on by unscrupulous lawyers more interested in a fee than in the future happiness of their client.

While alimony may be a financial drain on the man, all too often it is the woman who pays the higher price, psychologically. Since the usual stipulation in alimony arrangements holds that payments cease when the wife remarries, she now has a strong motive for never remarrying but remaining locked in an unproductive and essentially destructive relationship with a man she no longer loves.

"Why should I get married again?" one ex-wife asked. "My alimony allows me to live in high style. I have plenty of men to take me out and I don't intend giving up the weekly check even if I find someone I love."

One ex-wife remained unmarried for fifteen years after her divorce in order not to sacrifice alimony payments. It was only when she realized how poor a substitute for marriage were the regular checks that she could find a man and remarry. Rather than a blessing, alimony often turns into a curse, especially if the alimony is for a substantial amount and prospective suitors do not have equal financial resources.

The Widowed

When a mate is lost through death rather than legal action, the situation is different from that following separation or divorce. Some go through a period of mourning as is natural and to be expected after the loss of a loved one, and then remarry, frequently with happy results. Others, for one reason or another, find it impossible ever to establish another relationship. They may rationally decide they do not want to marry again and arrange their life in such a manner as to find it satisfactory, perhaps not as satisfactory as with the lost loved one, but still a reasonable adaptation to a new life.

But some are unable to readjust to the death of a mate. They remain closely tied to the departed, believing this due to deep love. As a rule, those who enjoyed their marriage find it easier to remarry than those who found marriage a trying time. It is interesting that here, too, statistics show that widows have a better chance of remarrying, no matter at what age, than those women who have never married. It is no longer considered unusual to hear of women in their fifties, sixties, and even seventies, remarrying. One man was delighted when his mother, who became a widow at seventy-two, married again within two years.

"That proves her life with my father was a good one," he said, "and she had no trouble, because she had been happy, in finding someone her own age with whom to share the rest of her life."

Sometimes real complications deter remarriage. For one, there may be the presence of children. It takes a man or woman of some emotional maturity to accept children not their own. It is a denial of truth to believe that this is a simple matter. It is a problem of remarriage that is not unmanageable but may need much discussion between the prospective husband and wife and exploration of each other's feelings about the children and themselves in order that both may be able to deal with it wisely.

Another problem some widows face is that of fortune hunters. As women are now outliving men and often are left with substantial sums of money, they frequently become fearful of the motives of sudden suitors. There is no advantage to a woman in a marrying a man whose only interest is to fleece her of her inheritance, but on the other hand there is no advantage in remaining alone because she possesses more money than the man who wishes to marry her. It is not difficult for anyone of average intelligence to distinguish between an opportunistic fortune hunter and sincere affection, if one does not wish to be deceived.

One widow past sixty, who had been left a comfortable amount of money by her husband, met a man three years younger, not nearly as wealthy. Despite the warnings of well-intentioned friends she married him and, to the chagrin of these same friends, soon proved to be even happier than with her first husband. The second husband was devoted to her, proud of her, and made no secret of his affection. She, on the other hand, was happy to make life easier for him which she could well afford to do.

It is important for the separated, the divorced, and the widowed to remember that while they may have suffered the loss of someone they love, this need not mark the end of life. If they have courage, they can tackle the changes forced upon them by the vicissitudes of living.

When mourning for someone who has died lasts beyond the traditional year, it may be regarded as containing feelings other than pure sorrow. A protracted mourning, involving a withdrawal from life and worshiping at the shrine of the lost relationship, means that the death has not been accepted, that the one who mourns feels angry, resentful, and perhaps guilty, but essentially the grief is centered on the self.

Living entails dealing with ever-changing circumstances anyway, not such drastic ones, perhaps, as divorce and death, but changes that require a constant spirit of bravery. There are the dramatic heroes of the battlefields but there are also heroes and heroines, in far greater numbers, who in quiet bravery live out the wars within themselves.

14 SEX IS FOR PLEASURE

How we first learn "the facts of life," as they are realistically called, influences our later attitude toward sex.

Many modern parents know they are supposed to answer a child's questions about sex in a way that will not frighten the child. They will sit down with him when he asks questions and carefully explain the functions of the sexual organs in reproduction and other once taboo subjects.

But there is one thing most parents do not point out. They forget to mention that sex can be fun, especially with someone you love.

One reason they do not speak of pleasure is that they fear if they stress this aspect of sex the child will instantly set out to indulge in sexual activity, for most children are not as yet prepared to pass by a pleasure.

But this fear is misplaced, for whether or not the parent mentions the fact that sex is an intensely exciting experience, this is already known to the child either from discovery of the pleasurable potentials of his own body, from friends, his fantasies, or his reading.

Another reason why pleasure in sex may not be brought up by a parent is that he may have difficulty in his own life accepting sex as pleasurable. This the child will sense, for even if there is no direct communication about sex, the child will discover attitudes that exist in his parents without their ever needing to say even a word that relates to sex.

What is called "nonverbal" communication is as important to the child as the spoken word. The parent who draws back in distaste or fear from the loving embrace of a child is discouraging the pleasurable aspects of physical contact more surely than the strictest of moral lectures. Just as damaging may be the parent who is starved for sexual affection in his own life and expresses his hunger through seductive behavior toward the child, which may arouse unmanageable emotions in the child and create for him an aura of danger and anxiety about his own sexual responses.

Some parents seem unaware of the effect of their actions on a child. During a consultation with a psychiatrist, one father whose fifteen-year-old daughter was getting help because of severe personality difficulties, was cautioned about the danger of overdemonstrative behavior toward his daughter.

The father listened seriously and promised to be more careful in the future. However, as he left the psychiatrist's office and met his daughter in the waiting room by prearrangement, he threw his arms around her and kissed her on the lips in a manner more typical of a fiancé than a loving, protective father. When, during a future consultation, the psychiatrist called this to his attention, he seemed genuinely unaware of the implications in this sort of behavior.

It is sometimes difficult for parents to give comfortable, spontaneous warmth, walking the narrow line between detachment and being unduly provocative of the child's sexual feelings, which are far more easily aroused than most adults realize. Sexual feelings in a child are very open. He learns to hide and deny them only as he grows up. Small children are very free in their curiosity about sex which to them is a natural field of inquiry.

The Importance of Tenderness

Those unable to love sometimes use sex for many other purposes besides pleasure. Lacking the ability to be tender, some use it in the interests of anger. Sex becomes an attack, rather than a loving embrace. One man whose wife was better educated than he, and who felt that when she discussed subjects of an intellectual nature she was deliberately trying to be superior to him, would, as revenge, force her to submit to certain practices in sexual intimacy which she considered degrading. He was showing his anger, in part deserved, since she sometimes made a display of her knowledge in his presence with such snide remarks as "he wouldn't be interested in this," which implied his intellectual inferiority.

One woman would sometimes refuse intimacy with her husband, alternating with periods in which her demands would be so excessive that it was impossible for him to gratify them. She would then wonder out loud, in front of him, how she could possibly be interested in a man who possessed so weak a sexual drive. She expressed her hostility at men and at her husband through both these techniques, first by refusing him and then by attempting to prove he was sexually inferior.

As in infidelity, some engage in sexual intimacy with husbands or wives far above their actual need to reassure themselves of masculinity or femininity. Thus, some men demand sexual gratification not so much for pleasure but in an attempt to prove to their wives and themselves that they are "real he-men." Ironically, such attempts may end in a more limited capacity for sex than if they made love only when they felt genuinely moved.

There are men capable of making love several times in one night, night after night after night. It may be surprising that such men frequently find only a minimum of satisfaction in this display of sexual prowess. Often the ability to have repeated orgasms is due to the feeling that none of the orgasms is really satisfactory because of the lack of a deep, warm feeling for the women.

The same is true for women whose capacity for orgasms seems unlimited. Some of these women boast of this capacity only as long as they do not meet a man who is their match. When they do come up against such a man, their capacity suddenly becomes severely limited. A woman who formerly complained no man could satisfy her, when she met a lover who was more capable of satisfying her than the men she had known previously, changed her complaint to one about his excessive demands.

Another use of sex is as solace, as comfort at times one feels despairing and lonely. Or it may be used as a tranquilizer. Feeling tense, perhaps unable to sleep, some use the anxiety-reducing function of sex as the primary reason for intercourse. While the reduction of anxiety is a welcome byproduct of a good sexual relationship, it cannot be made the chief aim without diminishing the pleasure one receives and gives. Anxiety, if present in large degree, blocks many of our joyful responses.

There are those who attempt to use sex to prove how free and liberal they are. They but deceive themselves if this is their reason, for they protest too much. One is free about sex only when one engages in it out of true desire for someone, not to prove something.

As one newly married wife told her husband, "For the first time in my life I feel it is *you* I want, not sex."

Some claim they indulge in sex just to give the other pleasure. One wife told a friend she dutifully "had sex" with her husband three times a week without enjoying it. But, she added, she did not mind because it gave him so much pleasure. She was using sex to ingratiate herself with her husband. Ingratiation takes its psychic toll eventually on both the one guilty of it and the one who allows it to be thrown his way, for the hidden anger is sensed even though covered up.

This wife had been raised in such a way that she believed sexual satisfaction was purely a masculine prerogative, that the woman should be subservient and expect no pleasure for herself. When sexual intimacy is undertaken thus out of a sense of duty, the partner as well fails to find it a very delightful adventure. To the sensitive person, true enjoyment requires a mutuality that is absent when one "does" it for the other.

Some women will, on occasion however, find pleasure, if not full sexual satisfaction, in meeting their husband's needs out of love for him at a time when they themselves may not feel very desirous of sex. The biological differences between the sexes is such that women are capable of helping a man achieve sexual satisfaction without receiving any, unlike men who cannot perform satisfactorily if they are not aroused.

When Sex Is Spiritless

Much of the literature describing sexual relations has attempted to isolate the technique of giving and receiving sexual satisfaction from the emotional relationship that is necessary for full satisfaction. Many writers seem to proceed on the assumption that all one needs is a technical know-how to promptly destroy all difficulties and transform every frigid wife into an amalgam of the fabled beauties of history and Hollywood, and every impotent husband into a veritable Casanova. Here, too, the modern emphasis on technical proficiency results in a spiritless, mechanical performance rather than a joyful, rich uniting of man and woman.

It is unfortunate that many of these sexual "how-to" manuals are written from a masculine point of view and approach the art of marital love with the same cold competence as found in a manual on how to repair a television set.

One woman, complaining about her husband's lack of tenderness, declared, "Every time he makes love to me I can see the paragraph in the marriage manual he is following at that moment."

What has not been stressed sufficiently is the emotion which must exist between two people for them to find sex truly satisfactory. The act of sex contains the essence of their feeling for each other, often a compound of sensuality, affection, tenderness, respect, and friendship.

If affectionate feelings are not present, sex is apt to be forced, harsh, unfeeling. One woman said, "My husband is always hurling himself at me, almost as if he was being impelled by some force outside him, rather than flowing into me. He rushes me so that rarely do I have the chance to know what I feel. He dances so beautifully and smoothly, why can't he understand that sex should be like a lovely dance, equally smooth, graceful and rhythmic, rather than hard, awkward, and thrusting?"

The "smooth, graceful and rhythmic" feelings to which she refers doubtless come out of the warm, tender rapport between two people who have deep affection for each other. But there are infinite varieties of taste and some women find a strong, firm approach more appealing.

We cannot be tender to order. Tenderness cannot be demanded like a ham and cheese sandwich. It may be blocked in some men because of fear of women or fear of their own sexual feelings. In others exists the fear that to be tender is somehow to make themselves vulnerable to hurt. They hide their anxiety behind a gruff physical exterior in which tenderness finds no place.

There are some women who are repelled by what they feel an excess of tenderness, just as there are men who find it difficult to make love to a woman whose sexual receptivity is too obvious. The essential problem is for the partners to be sensitive to each other's needs. Those who are emotionally strong are the ones who can best meet the needs of a mate rather than force the mate to meet their needs.

One sign of strength is to understand that the sexual needs of the other may be different from one's own. It is uncommon for any two people, no matter how much in love or how well matched, each time they make love to have precisely the same degree of wanting each other at precisely the same moment. In the good marriage each makes a serious effort to fulfill the other's needs. But if there is drastic difference in needs, there may ensue trouble that both must make an effort to overcome, with or without psychological guidance.

Marriages Are Not Made in Bed

One difference may be the amount of time each requires in preparation for sexual intimacy. Some think the preparation is limited to the minutes immediately preceding intercourse. The happy marriage is not made in bed. It is a product of the entire aura of living. The husband who comes home from work and devotes the evening to pursuits of his own, scarcely speaking to his wife, cannot understand why, even though he does everything the sex manual commands, his wife acts cool to him when he tries to embrace her. He does not realize that had he been more friendly during the evening, she might have felt more receptive.

Similarly, the wife who has nagged all through supper may find herself disappointed when her husband does not wax duly romantic as the lights go off. Anger and sexual desire usually do not make good bedfellows.

If sexual intimacy grows out of a couple's whole life together, it becomes the spontaneous expression of the closeness of a man and woman rather than an ordered and prescribed ritual. There will be less possibility of the intrusion of emotions that interfere with spontaneity, such as rage, fear, or distrust.

One woman who entered marriage fully endowed with what she believed healthy sexual needs, found much of her pleasure destroyed by her husband's constant questions every time they went to bed. He would ask her to tell him about her previous experiences with men.

Some husbands plague their wives by attempts to third-degree them about former lovers at a time which should be devoted not to such lurid research but to an intensification of one's pleasurable feelings. The reasons for this curiosity are varied. Some men need to feel jealous, to compete with others in the life of their mate in order to become sexually stimulated. They want their wives to declare them superior lovers (in their unconscious they are still competing with their father for their mother).

Others find it difficult to believe that women, too, possess strong sexual desires and by insisting the women recount other sexual experiences they become reassured about the existence of female sexuality and feel more accepted themselves sexually (they still have remnants of a fear of the woman).

No Female "Peeping Toms"

Still others need social stimulation. Most of us have had the experience of not feeling particularly hungry until we sit down to a meal with others, when the stimulation of watching them eat will whet our appetite. Similarly, some men and women find the thought of others engaging in intercourse sexually exciting. It is for this reason that novels, plays, and movies on erotic subjects are sexually stimulating and, therefore, so repulsive to those who do not wish to be, or are incapable of being, so stimulated or who fear their own sexual feelings.

There seems to be quite a difference between what stimulates men and women. In general, men are the more open voyeurs, finding the experience of observation exciting, which women do less frequently. There are no burlesque shows where men slowly undrape their bodies for the titillation of female audiences who egg them on by shrieking, "Take it off, take it off!"

There are no magazines which feature the nude male torso for the benefit of the lonely woman reader. It also is almost unknown for a female Peeping Tom to be arrested.

Women, on the other hand, are aroused by a different set of stimuli. Stories of love and romance more often serve to excite them, rather than pictures of naked men. Scenes of tenderness are usually much more sexually stirring to the female than pornography, which finds its major market among males.

Good Sex Is Emotional as Well as Physical

Freudian psychoanalysts believe that there are three major stages to our psychosexual life—the oral stage, when we are babies, in which the mouth is the pleasurable center of our

universe; the anal stage, when we first learn to control our
bodily functions which up until then have given us pleasure
at will; and the genital stage, where sexual pleasure finally
reposes chiefly in the genitals, which is the stage of maturity.

Good genital sex means not only reaching the physical stage
but the emotional development requisite to the achievement
of full physical enjoyment. Sex, it is believed, can be completely enjoyed only by those who are fairly mature emotionally, who are not using the act of sex for other reasons
than pleasure.

Among the deterrents to harmonious, mature sex are fear,
anger, and guilt. These emotions, if so excessive that one
cannot handle them to prevent their interfering with his
sexual life, may be symptoms of emotional immaturity.

One important component of good sex, which may surprise some, is the quality of friendship and companionship.
Liking, as well as loving, is found in the happy marriage.
You usually have to like someone to be able to be tender
toward him, and without any tenderness there is no mature
love.

There is also found in happily married couples a feeling
of playfulness in sex, a sense of fun and laughter at times.
Rather than a burden, sex to them is often a gay game. But if
there is great anger between a husband and wife, it is impossible, of course, to express merriment or laughter.

When a man or woman is unable to achieve much pleasure
out of sex, even though he or she tries time and again, it
might be advisable to seek psychological help. It is tragic to
think of how many go through life without ever realizing
their potential for sexual enjoyment. This has nothing to do
with the number of orgasms, but with the richness of the feeling for oneself and the other person.

One man who felt crippled sexually decided to seek psychological help. He was unable to become sexually intimate with his wife and could only be aroused with what he described as "sick excitement" when other men kissed her or caressed her casually in public. That was the full extent of his sexual feelings.

Among other experiences he uncovered from childhood during his psychiatric treatment was recollection of a scene when he was eight years old. He had walked in on his mother and father in bed and seen his father fondling his mother's breast. He remembered becoming very aroused sexually and then feeling great guilt. He feared his father's wrath should he know how his son felt. He had been suffering this guilt for years, a psychic albatross around his neck.

He became aware that he was reliving the same situation with his wife in that his guilt prevented him from being potent with her (in his unconscious she represented the forbidden mother) but he could not keep himself from becoming stimulated when other men caressed her, as his father had his mother. Actually, he realized he sought to place his wife in such situations as though to re-enact the original traumatic scene which had troubled him but also excited him.

How To Destroy Desire

Some women may need help because of the subtle ways they have, of which they are usually unaware, of destroying a man's sexual desire as they unconsciously seek to castrate him. They do not realize that trying to control his behavior during the sexual act (at other times, too) is a form of castration. They convey to him the feeling that he is not acceptable sexually by such remarks as "Must we?" or "I'm tired tonight," when he suggests sexual intimacy.

Or when he says, "Wasn't that wonderful?" after intimacy,

they will deprecate him by shrugging their shoulders and declaring casually, "It was all right." Or perhaps while he is making love they will yawn and urge, "Hurry up, I want to watch Perry Como." Or they will insist, or somehow make him feel, he should not have an orgasm until they are ready, as they try to control him even unto his final pleasure. All these feelings are experienced as contempt and anger by the partner (a man may do the same to his wife).

There are a number of men who will take such animadversions in their stride and continue to enjoy sexual pleasure little affected by their wives' problems. A group of psychologically sophisticated men were eating lunch, when one of them expressed, as men will do, a desire for sexual intimacy with the charming hostess.

The man next to him asked, "Why would you want that castrating female?"

The first man replied quietly, "What do I care about her fantasies? I would enjoy her anyway."

Too often both men and women seek to excuse their own sexual problems by blaming their partner, rather than exploring their own difficulties.

Then there is the man or woman who is rigid about the number of times per week or month they will indulge in sexual intimacy. Some men feel they must save energy for their work. Some women limit the times as a way of control. Such compulsive behavior tells of a fear of being free about sexual feelings. Sex is not a numbers game, except for the frightened.

All Is Fair in Forepleasure

Some believe there is only one proper way to make love, with the woman lying beneath the man, sensation confined to the penis and vagina. All else is deemed obscene and abnormal. In emotionally mature men and women the final gratification comes from the genital organs but forepleasure may consist of pleasurable sensations being aroused in other parts of the body. Nothing is perversion if it is used not as the aim of the sexual act but as a means of increasing excitement. Perversion occurs only when forepleasure becomes the end, as with those who seek substitute gratification to the point that they are incapable of orgasm through the normal culmination in intercourse.

Some authorities believe there are times when masturbation in marriage is justified, if, for instance, a husband and wife must be apart for a long period. They hold that the relief provided by masturbation is merely a substitute for the sexual intimacy desired with the mate and preferable to plunging into an affair with someone else, which would be far more damaging to the marriage.

If, however, the mate is available and masturbation is preferred, this is unusual. There are some instances, although rare, where emotional disturbance runs so deep that a husband or wife will masturbate, or threaten to masturbate, rather than give of themselves to the other. This often comes across to the mate as the height of hostility even though it may be inspired by an awful fear of the opposite sex.

Such agonized souls are trying to obtain the only sexual pleasure of which they are capable, one carried over from childhood. They prefer to cling desperately to masturbation, getting greater satisfaction out of the fantasies that accompany it (it is the fantasy, incidentally, that may cause the guilt over masturbation rather than the act itself) than to risk the responsibility inherent in possessing or being possessed sexually by someone else.

They are to be pitied, for no one chooses consciously to live this deeply in fantasy and thus dwarf his sexuality. When this happens, the early life of such a person may have held such alarming fears that he cannot face the reality of loving another. His fears, wishes, and guilts may be too intense to allow him to be sexually free with anyone. He may still be too entangled in the secret guilts of childhood.

Much has been written about the role of the woman in the sexual act. Should she ever be the aggressor? Is it proper for her to make advances if she feels sexually aroused?

Of course it is, as long as she feels comfortable in doing so. There are times she may wish intimacy when her husband may not particularly care to instigate it but certainly will not object in the least to caresses that arouse him. Some couples take turns in being the one to lead the way to sex, although generally the man is the initiator. It is harmful only if a man completely depends on his wife to arouse him, if he needs her to be the aggressor all the time. In many cases where this is so, his resentment against his own passivity eventually breaks out and overrides all other feelings, destroying or harming the relationship.

There are no ironclad rules about sex. Each one, man or woman, should do what he feels like doing and what his love for the other inspires him to do.

If two people love each other, it is less likely that they will act in a way that is destructive to themselves or the other. Sometimes when there is an effort to comply with the wishes of the beloved, one often finds pleasure where none was expected. This is one of the rewards of mutuality.

15 THE MYSTIQUE OF
THE ORGASM

One of the major discoveries of the middle twentieth century seems to be the orgasm.

The literature, both belles lettristic and scientific, of longer ago than thirty years—except for Ovid and his poetic description of the mutual orgasm—for the most part seems to have neglected what has today become to many a major preoccupation.

Many men and women who would not dream of discussing their bank account or their salary seem to have little compunction about sailing off into the most detailed descriptions of their orgasms, both satisfactory and unsatisfactory, and all that led up to them.

At a recent cocktail party one young woman, in talking of a discarded lover, said thoughtfully, "All he ever did for me was to give me one perfect orgasm. Great though it felt, I hardly think it was worth giving up six months of my life for that!"

Some suffer acute misery in their search for the elusive

orgasm, described so vividly in recent books as shaking the earth, exploding like skyrockets, and creating an indissoluble bond between two people who can reach the pyrotechnic climax simultaneously.

To these poets of the orgasm, the act of achieving mutuality to the split second takes on mystical importance of a religious quality similar to the experience of being "saved." Some fanatical devotees even believe that the world's major problems stemming from hostility, such as war and dictatorship, could be solved if only orgastic potency could be reached by all of suffering humanity, but especially by its leaders. (It might be revealing to study the sexual adequacy of leaders, à la Kinsey, with all identities protected, of course.)

A cult started by the late Dr. Wilhelm Reich revolved around the belief that the orgasm was "the" cure for all neurosis. Men and women sat in an "orgone box" which gave off blue rays that magically brought potency to them. The box may have helped to relieve their guilt slightly, in that someone was thus sanctioning sex, but there is little proof that it solved any of the inner conflicts causing the inadequate sexual life.

There is very little evidence that the orgasm, pleasurable though it may be, plays a key role in human destiny. Its presence or lack is certainly important to our lives, but undue concern about it is merely a symptom of deeper problems. Like most things, it becomes vital only when one does not possess it.

A woman divorced two husbands because she was not satisfied with the quality of the sexual climax she reached with them. While this masked other motives, the overvaluation she placed upon the experience of orgasm contributed greatly to her decision to divorce. It is probable she would face the same problem with any man she chose.

What is the orgasm? In the male it is usually coincidental with the ejaculation of semen, following sexual excitation. With the female, it seems to serve no direct biological function but is the period of most intense sexual feeling climaxed by rhythmic involuntary contractions of the vagina, similar to the involuntary rhythmic contractions of the penis which usually accompany ejaculation.

The word "usually" is used because there are some instances where the male ejaculation is not accompanied by orgasm and where orgasms, as in preadolescent boys, are not accompanied by ejaculation. Secretion of fluid is not a necessary accompaniment of female orgasm.

Orgasms may be felt in different ways. Sometimes there is sensation primarily in the genital region. Sometimes the whole body is awakened and there is the feeling of being stirred from the toes to the furthermost hair of the head. Sometimes the orgasm is fierce, sometimes gentle. Sometimes it is so excruciatingly pleasurable that one feels transported out of this world. Sometimes it is sad and women burst into tears or men feel like crying. Sometimes it is casual, or playful, or even engaged in out of a sense of duty. It need not be "a grande passion" every time.

Some women experience the orgasm only in their clitoris, the tiny, pleasure-giving erectile organ between the vulva, or lips of the genital area, corresponding to the male penis. Others do not experience a marked climax as such but merely a strong rise in erotic feeling followed by sudden relaxation and sense of calm

A Capricious Division

There has been much discussion about the varieties of orgastic experience in the woman. Some writers have created a hierarchy of orgasm, insisting that the only true orgasm be considered the one experienced in the vagina as the result of the presence of the penis. Such writers consider the orgasm felt in the clitoris as of distinctly inferior variety. Yet there are women who experience vaginal orgasm as a result of clitoral stimulation, just as there are some who experience clitoral orgasm as a result of stimulation of the vagina.

To other authorities this division between vaginal and clitoral orgasm seems capricious. They believe that the important thing is the pleasure the woman experiences and her freedom from frustration after the completion of the act, for to be sexually aroused and not able to have an orgasm is felt by some as the height of adult frustration.

These authorities point out that some women who never have an explosive climax but do reach a certain pitch of excitement followed by a relaxed feeling, will find their sexual relations quite satisfactory until someone informs them they are being deprived. Such authorities are also inclined to believe that the means of achieving the orgasm, as long as it does not consist of antisocial behavior such as beatings, rape, or pathological exhibitionism, are immaterial. In their eyes, there is no such thing as sexual perversion when it takes place between a man and woman as forepleasure or does not involve severe pain.

Pernicious Sexual Propaganda

One of the most pernicious bits of propaganda put forth by the orgasm worshipers is that, to be worthwhile, orgasms must be simultaneous and mutual. To such worshipers, if either man or woman dares to experience an orgasm before the other, this is viewed with as much horror as the defilement of an idol by a religious Hindu.

In an effort to achieve this mutual, simultaneous orgasm, some couples destroy their chance for genuine pleasure. Pleasurable sex requires the letting go of controls so that one may experience the full intensity of one's emotions. For that reason, some lovers close their eyes or put out all the lights or turn off the television set or radio.

But if couples are deliberately working to achieve mutual orgasm, they must be constantly alert to the other's response and this diminishes awareness of their own feelings. It also increases self-consciousness which seems to cut down seriously one's capacity for enjoyment. Self-consciousness is an extremely contagious emotion so that the other's pleasure also becomes decreased.

Some men and women have difficulty feeling free enough to give up the controls they must relinquish momentarily in order to experience genital sex. This fear of letting go may trace back to the childhood fear of letting go in urination and defecation, in defiance of what, to a child, is the first sexual prohibition in life.

Children are warned they will lose the love of their parents if they do not control their urinary and bowel functions. It is a pleasurable feeling for a child to urinate and defecate and he must learn to restrain and control this pleasure to please his parents. If training has been too strict, all future sexual pleasure, which involves a letting go, will hold the same forbidden feeling. Any intense fear felt in the early sexual stages may carry over to the more advanced sexual stages.

Some adults, for instance, feel deep shame about defecation and urination, considering it embarrassing and disgusting to perform such functions in front of, or within the hearing of, a member of the opposite sex. They never feel comfortable in marriage unless they can use a bathroom in the far corner of the house, where they feel isolated, or perhaps, if their fear is too great, they never marry. One woman confessed that she felt far greater shame over urinating in a bathroom where a man could hear her than she did in having intercourse with him.

Some women place so much value on the orgasm that they even pretend to have one so the man will believe they are experiencing it. This is harmful to the woman, for the very feeling that she must simulate makes it that much more difficult for her to relax enough for a true orgasm.

The Joy of Taking Graciously

If one is engaging in sex for pleasure, not to demonstrate superior capacity to give or receive orgasms, or for any other of myriad unhappy reasons, he will concentrate on his own delight, knowing that the greatest joy he can give his partner is for him to find the experience a gratifying one.

If he is able to enjoy his own feelings, he will not become victim of an anger that usually arises when we make our own pleasure subservient to the pleasure of another. Some men attempt to withhold their orgasm for an inordinately long time after effecting an entrance because they feel they must wait for the woman, and this may affect their enjoyment of the sexual act. They become angry at what they feel a demand by the woman for them to hold back on their own gratification, although it may be their own conscience that is restricting them.

This does not apply to forepleasure, which may take as long as each desires. Here again, there are no rules, either of what forepleasure should consist, or the time it should consume. A common criticism by women is that men do not spend enough time in forepleasure for them to become fully aroused. If there are tender, warm feelings between a man and woman, they frequently seem to know almost intuitively what the other needs to achieve the most pleasure, or are able to discuss freely whatever problems they may experience in the mutual act and thus attempt to clear them up.

Some find themselves spinning conscious fantasies during sexual intimacy. One woman said she could achieve orgasm only by imagining she was an innocent slave girl in a harem and her husband the sultan she was forced to please. Another woman, during intercourse, would think of herself as a prostitute and her husband as one of her married customers. One man spoke of his need to imagine his wife a prostitute each time they had sex.

Some authorities believe such fantasies do no harm, that if they enable the person more easily to reach an orgasm, they serve a good purpose. Others, however, believe that these conscious fantasies hide deeper unconscious ones which should be faced to permit the person to feel free enough about his sexual feelings so he does not need to disguise them. They also believe the fantasies, both the ones of which he is aware and the deeper, hidden ones, keep him from being able to appreciate his partner fully. The fantasies are a smoke screen which prevent one from knowing and enjoying his mate and the sexuality that comes out of their love for each other. If one has to pretend the mate is someone else, one is denying the mate's existence as a person in his own right.

It is not necessary for the number of orgasms between husband and wife to be equally matched. Cost-accounting is not a valuable adjunct to love. Some women have two or three orgasms to the man's one, perhaps both clitoral and vaginal, while some men have several ejaculations to the woman's one orgasm. The pacing of each may vary and this is another difference it is important to accept.

If sometimes intercourse does not result in an orgasm for

either partner, there is no reason to believe the marriage is wrecked. In the eternity of love lies more than enough time to arrive at sexual Nirvana. It is essential to keep this in mind during the early days of adjustment in a marriage, for some women take weeks, months, perhaps even years of living with a man to reach the experience of fullest orgasm.

"Just Let Yourself Be"

Even after a pattern of orgasm has been worked out, there will be times it is not reached. The man or woman may be weary physically or psychologically. This is no reason, again, to exhaust oneself in its pursuit. Every experience need not achieve perfection and occasional failure only makes the successes that much sweeter.

One husband, always most careful to make sure that his wife reached an orgasm every time they became intimate, at the same time found that despite his thoughtfulness, his wife usually seemed far less interested than he in making love. He started to worry less about her orgasms, permitting himself release at his pleasure and to his wonder, this experience, which he had previously considered failure on his part, resulted in her wanting him as often as he did her.

Talking over a sexual problem with a mate may help in its resolution. One wife felt mired in an insoluble sexual dilemma. She did not want to have an orgasm before her husband because she then found it painful to continue the intercourse so he could reach a climax. She could not have an orgasm after him because she would not ask him to offer further cooperation (most men are only too happy to oblige their wives, either by remaining within her or assisting manually or orally, or both). She felt that mutual orgasm was too precarious to depend on for sustained satisfaction.

Her husband, with whom she finally discussed her di-lemma, suggested casually, without becoming upset, that she try to have an orgasm as a result of his ejaculation, stimulated by it.

"How can I do that?" she asked in surprise.

"Just let yourself be," he explained.

This is probably the single most important piece of advice that any man can give a woman in search of an orgasm. It cannot be worked for, it cannot be wished for, it is best achieved by just feeling free enough to let it happen. This implies, of course, a fair acceptance of the self and one's sexual feelings.

While at first extremely dubious about her husband's ad-vice, when he continued not to be worried about her but to enjoy his own pleasure, the wife discovered to her amazement that when she could "just let it happen," it did.

Where there is affection, each partner is only too happy to increase the other's satisfaction. He will willingly wait if occasionally the other does not, at the moment, feel like mak-ing love, not taking it as rejection but knowing the satisfac-tion will be greater for both because of the waiting.

The one who lives fully does not live for the orgasm. It is not a matter of life and death to him that he have one every so often or every time he makes love. He prefers to feel that it comes out of the desire of both himself and his mate rather than that it is a demand on either one's part. He is not ob-sessed with sex for sex's sake. He is not preoccupied with sex, but with thoughtfulness about his mate. He takes it for granted there will be eventual gratification, knowing there is likely to be far more gratification if he does not demand it.

Again, there are no rules—each according to his sexual needs. Tastes vary. Some men find desirable the very body odors that offend others who prefer that their wives use perfume. Some wives like to take a bath before sexual intimacy or ask their husbands to bathe, while others are much more comfortable when there is no bathing ritual. Some women do not like having intercourse during menstruation, while others do not mind it or even find it especially exciting.

Is sexual intimacy during menstruation dangerous, as some have charged? The preponderance of medical opinion seems to be that the only objection is on an esthetic basis. Psychologically, on the part of both man and woman, the blood may activate the fear of injury to the sexual organs, based on remnants of childhood sexual guilt. Many women become their most passionate during this period, however, and it would seem that if couples do not find it too unattractive, there is no danger in engaging in sexual intimacy.

One couple, before intercourse, always play strip poker. Another enjoy a few drinks together. Still others find movies, or plays, or dancing stimulating, while some prefer a period of quiet during which they read or listen to music.

Those who enjoy each other sexually are the ones, of course, who usually have little need to be unfaithful. They do not deny their attraction occasionally to members of the opposite sex, but they feel no overwhelming urge to become intimate with anyone but the mate who fulfills all their realistic needs.

There seems to be apparent contradiction in emphasizing that love should be a gift, yet in the sexual act each partner should be intent on achieving his own pleasure. This contradiction is more apparent than real, for the greatest gift we can bestow on someone we love is for us to reach the heights of pleasure because they are near. If, through our love of them and their love of us, we possess moments of richness within ourselves possible no other way, we can pay them no greater tribute.

It is amazing but true, that when we feel depressed or unhappy, this feeling is communicated in a flash so fast it makes rocket travel look like stagecoach, to those close to us who, almost by osmosis, then become plunged into the same despair.

Pleasure works the same way. A happy person exudes an air that promptly inspires anyone near him to feel happy. If he treats someone else as lovable, that person responds in kind.

The one whose mate finds deep pleasure in the love embrace receives that pleasure as a cherished gift. There is no better way, possibly no other way, to make someone we love happy, than through our own happiness.

Most of us seem to be engaged in the struggle between our search for the ideal and the suspicion that we are incapable of attaining that ideal. Marriage, as an extremely emotional, intimate relationship, is frequently a focal point of this self-imposed task of trying to reach divinity with feet we feel are hopelessly clay-encased.

Aware of defects and deficiencies in ourselves, many of us enter marriage in the hope that first, this sanctified state will magically correct our defects and deficiencies, and second, that we will have another chance at life by creating something perfect.

Even if it were possible for human beings to create perfection, it is questionable whether this would be a happy outcome. There are few things more tiresome than absolute perfection. It is for that reason that man-made art is far preferable to most sensitive viewers than machine-made perfection. The mole on the face of a beautiful woman as an imperfection adds interest and enhances her loveliness.

A not very realistic young wife boasted to an older and

wiser friend, "Our marriage is ideal. We are perfectly suited to each other. We have never had one quarrel. And we are determined to keep it that way."

The friend cynically replied, "Better find some trouble, honey, or you'll end in the divorce court."

Perhaps it is no accident that after some marriages break up, friends of the couple exclaim, "But it seemed like such a perfect marriage!"

A marriage where husband and wife feel they have to work to keep it "absolutely perfect" bears an almost unendurable strain. There should be the flexibility of humanness in marriage. Steel is strong because it is a flexible material while cast iron breaks more easily because it is not.

Human beings, at least thus far along in civilization, do not appear compatible with perfection. The attempt to achieve the more-than-human often results in the less-than-human. Some of the worst tyrants in history, from Torquemada to Hitler, were intent on achieving the perfect state. Similarly, some of the most tyrannical mates are those who strive for the perfect marriage or to be the perfect husband or wife.

Human beings are interesting, exciting, challenging—but not perfect. There seems little chance we will ever be perfect, or that marriage will be perfect, or that sex will be perfect, or that children will be perfect no matter how many times Dr. Spock is read.

In discussing a cooperative colony that failed, one of those who took part in it explained the failure was due not to drones who did not perform their full share of the work but to the fiercely relentless workers who attempted to turn the colony into a heaven on earth and would be satisfied with nothing less. Similarly, in marriage, the mate who demands perfection and works at it with might and main is frequently the one who forces the ultimate destruction of the marriage.

Being Human Means Imperfections

Satisfaction in marriage is related to how successfully the person accepts himself, according to a study of married couples conducted by Daniel Eastman, a psychologist. The man or woman who thinks little of himself tends to think little of his or her mate, Dr. Eastman found. How one feels about the self thus is reflected in how one feels about the world—loved ones, marriage, work.

The one who accepts himself is not afraid to be himself with someone he loves. He feels little need for defenses, he is not anxious, he does not need to pretend. He can permit his partner to see his frailties and know his partner will not criticize him for the shortcomings but accept them as part of his being human.

In such a relationship the intimacy grows even deeper over the years and sexual satisfaction becomes even more satisfying with time, rather than disappearing, as happens with those who must act on guard continually lest the other not love them because they are not perfect.

Psychoanalysts, psychiatrists, pyschologists, and marriage counselors stress over and over to those who come to them for help that marriage *cannot* be perfect. The need to strive for perfection in marriage usually comes out of the refusal to accept oneself as imperfect.

This unreal demand for perfection is caused by a number of forces which build up steam in early childhood. Children of demanding, overly conscientious parents are apt to adopt as their own the very values which made them suffer, and eventually make the same demands on themselves and their children as their parents once made on them.

The demand for perfection may also reflect an attempt to

emulate a parent who, during infancy, was seen as perfect. Many of those who make the demand that marriage be perfect are under the mistaken notion that their parents were perfect and their parents' marriage was perfect and fail to be satisfied by anything short of perfection for themselves, which means they will never be satisfied.

Others, who suffered by being raised by parents whose marriage was obviously unhappy, attempt to make up for their past misery by trying to achieve an idealized marriage, as though to say angrily to their parents, "This is what your marriage *should* have been like so I would have been happier." They recoil from any flaw in their own marriage, believing it a sign the marriage will then be as doomed as their parents' marriage.

Such people may find it difficult to achieve happiness in marriage because their hostility toward their parents is so great that they permit themselves to be guided by only one feeling—their marriage will be everything that their parents' marriage was not. Little do they realize that rather than asserting independence, they are showing dependence on their parents by using them as a negative model out of hatred, which can be a far greater tie to parents than love, for love is apt to set one free.

Another reason for demanding perfection is that many of us were raised in an atmosphere of conditional love. Parents communicated to us the feeling we could be loved only if we were perfect little boys or girls. Our childhood thinking went: They want me to obey them and do everything they say and be perfect and then they will love me, otherwise they will hate me, so I will be perfect so they will love me, and everyone else must be perfect, too, or I will not love them.

One way in which people mistakenly strive for perfection is to try never to quarrel with each other. If we can drain off mild annoyance by expressing it before it builds up to intense anger, it obviously makes the chances for a successful marriage better than if we dam up anger until it bursts out in cataclysmic rage.

Some couples do manage, by exerting the highest of control, to live together without ever displaying a sign of fury. But it is natural for most people to engage in occasional arguments that clear the air. It is only when anger prevails most of the time that it becomes a destructive thing. This occurs when someone who himself is full of hatred sees the other as hostile but refuses to recognize his own hostility, sparing himself the greater pain of facing his own hatred which he represses and denies.

Self-Control as Part of Emotional Maturity

The person who angers easily and frequently is apt to be the one who asks the impossible of himself and others. He is impatient and intolerant of anything that does not go according to the way he thinks it should. He becomes furious if he or anyone else makes an error or fails to produce what he wants at the moment he wants it. He has little control of the self, little toleration of frustration.

Self-control, when it is conscious and comes out of our thinking through a situation so that we are not dominated by an impulse or whim, is part of emotional maturity. This is not to be confused with the rigid need for control that we see in some who are afraid to experience their emotions and clamp the lid on their capacity to feel anger or tenderness or sorrow or fear. They wear a mask of self-possession but actually are very little in possession of the self.

All marriages hold in them a certain amount of pain and frustration, for it is impossible to be deeply involved with another human being without making ourselves vulnerable to his ability to hurt us. Many of those who lead lives of bitter isolation are lonely through choice, to avoid the pain that accompanies close human contact.

The old maid or the bachelor is usually depicted as fussy and irritable, a stereotype which is in reality a recognition of an inability to bear frustration and a narcissistic attitude toward life. Ironically, by attempting to avoid making the compromises and renunciations necessary to live with others, they end up by depriving themselves of many of the pleasures that make living bearable.

In marriage, one has to give up some pleasure and learn to bear some frustration. It is unusual for any two people engaged in a mutual endeavor always to want the same thing at the same time and, therefore, one or both obviously has to surrender a number of his wishes. There are times, however, one can say "no" to a mate if one feels deeply about an issue. If there is trust, he will not love you less and may even love you more for your ability to take a firm stand. Disagreement by itself does not destroy a marriage, especially if it is made in the spirit of the free expression of one's feelings.

Most people find a marriage without children unsatisfying. Many find in their children the deepest meaning of the marital relationship. Yet it is impossible to bear children without pain, and the raising of children requires that parents deny themselves many pleasures. They have to sacrifice economically. They have to sacrifice a great deal of their freedom of movement, for they cannot let children fend for themselves. Yet, if they are not prepared to make these sacrifices and bear the pain, they will never achieve the joy and satisfaction of parenthood.

"Raising" literally means "lifting a burden." The raising of a child means lifting a burden from his shoulders, and feels also, at times, as though one were lifting a burden to his own shoulders. But men and women choose to do this when they get married and have children. While it is natural that they sometimes complain about the troubles involved in raising a family, it is not helpful to them or the children if they constantly castigate the children for being the burdens that all children necessarily are.

In investigating the difficulties a marriage is encountering, it is often useful to question husband and wife about their wish to have children. The refusal to have children often reflects a desire not to assume the responsibilities of maturity. If one mate is very intent on having a family and the other refuses, this can often be a source of serious conflict. Sometimes a wife is so hurt by her husband's refusal to give her a baby that she cannot even voice her disappointment, feeling that if he loved her, he would not need to be asked.

Lack of Perfection Starts at Home

In giving up the ideal of perfection, we must first give it up for ourselves. If we are unable to accept the lack of perfection in ourselves, we cannot accept it in those we would like to love but cannot, because we will not accept them as they are— imperfect.

Emotional maturity requires not only the ability to accept the pain and frustration the world imposes upon us but also the ability to accept the frustration of our wish for perfection. While never giving up the wish to progress, we must still be able to accept ourselves as we are.

Maturity is not the achieving of perfection, but the willingness to live with the imperfections of ourselves and those close to us. If we can do this, we have the chance of being happy and creating a happy home.

The mature person is able to acknowledge he is not divine and therefore he is subject to all the ignoble emotions of rage, envy, fear, avarice, and hate, as well as the more noble ones of love, understanding, and sympathy.

He accepts these same qualities of humanness in those around him, not demanding they be godlike. Unless he is able to do this, he will hate those traits in others which he finds repugnant in himself but is unable to admit he has.

Self-acceptance is not the same as conceit or egoism. The one who accepts himself is much less conceited than the willful, self-centered person who is lost in illusions about himself. The one who accepts himself knows his strengths and weaknesses, does not ask the impossible of himself or others but uses what resources he has as well as he can.

The inability to accept the so-called base emotions in the self is frequently related to the inability to accept one's own body and its natural functions. An attractive, talented woman in her late thirties, who had no difficulty in securing the attentions of eligible men, refused to marry any of them because, among other reasons, she felt that to live with a man would expose her to the shame of being seen without make-up, going to the bathroom, getting dressed and undressed. She thought her body disgusting and unpresentable to the human eye, even her own.

Thus, she usually became irritable and irascible with men to whom she felt most attracted, proving once again that the more we try to be like angels, the more we are apt to act like devils. She would not accept herself as a woman or as a human being.

"Emotional Maturity" Is Not Perfection

One of the problems about using the term "emotional maturity" is that the perfection-strivers will then, as some have done already, set this up as their goal, and in turn despise themselves not for being "imperfect" but for being "emotionally immature." In some circles, emotional immaturity is the sin of the day. Members of such groups do not denounce each other as "sinful" or "wicked" but speak with great scorn about those who are "emotionally immature."

It must be remembered that emotional maturity is not an end in itself but a process, a way of being, an attitude of growth nurtured by the awareness of self.

As Dr. Martin Grotjahn, psychoanalyst, puts it so eloquently in his book:*

Because modern man's knowledge of himself includes knowledge of his unconscious, he now demands more from himself than he had formerly. It is difficult to know oneself. It is almost impossible to be oneself. Either is a lifelong and creative assignment.

Some mythical goal of emotional maturity need not be reached before two people form a relationship, because the very relationship, if it is to be a happy one, will move in the direction of emotional maturity through mutual satisfactions. We achieve more complete self-realization as we are able to join with others, and through the mutual gratifications enhance awareness of self.

Marriage, having lost its original economic function, when it is a good marriage, has become essentially an institution for emotional security through psychological growth. A challenge to mature emotionally is offered automatically to everyone who says, "I do." In the days of primitive man, when merely to survive was a struggle, there was little time or need

* *Psychoanalysis and the Family Neurosis.* New York: W. W. Norton & Co., 1960.

to face the inner self. But now, the dangers of the jungle or of setting up a home in wild country as the pioneers in America did, are past and there are other dangers to be faced—the dangers inside ourselves. They need not be dangers if we know what to do about them.

To be successful in love and marriage requires that one be willing to head for a fair degree of emotional maturity. It is not enough to be physically and intellectually mature, for many who marry possess these two qualities but cannot live happily together.

An emotionally mature person is more likely to transfer some of the love of self, which we all possess as children, to another. He is more likely to give up a good share of his narrow selfishness. It would be unnatural, if not impossible, to be completely unselfish, and those who pretend to be are merely deceiving themselves, but we have to be able to consider the feelings and wishes of someone else as important as our own.

There is a considerable difference between unselfishness and masochism. Some wives pride themselves on how much they "do" for their husbands, boast how often they give up their own wishes to bow to their husband's desires. This is not unselfishness; it is rather a protest in reverse against "giving in" to their husband. Through their "see what a good girl am I" attitude, these wives may just be taking revenge on their husbands in other, far more subtle ways than outright attack.

Those able to love unselfishly are also the ones who, in turn, are more likely to be loved, for they make few demands. "Do you love me? Say you love me," a wife will beg her husband, needing the reassurance, demanding he love her. Chekov wrote that if we fear to lose something we have already lost it. Another way of looking at it is that if we fear to lose something, we wish to lose it.

The Meaning of Mature Love

The one able to love in responsible fashion has usually worked out for himself either consciously in words or thoughts, or unconsciously in attitudes, a wise philosophy of life. He has given up much of the magic of childhood wherein he expected his every wish to be carried out by an all-kind, all-understanding mother who only existed in his fantasy. He has successfully dealt with most of his childhood hatreds. He has accepted, then given up, many of his intense feelings for the parent of the opposite sex, natural at a certain age. He has usually relinquished much of the dependency he once felt on his mother and father.

He usually can act in other ways than primarily on the basis of childhood feelings that were appropriate between him and his parents. He is able to look at himself with a certain amount of objectivity and know what he feels. He does not need to hurl feelings, because they are unbearable at times, at others so that, as he mistakenly believes, he can escape the intensity of them.

Ideally any two people of the opposite sex about the same age, sharing a number of interests, should be able to live together in happiness. In reality, people possess so many emotional conflicts that many, even with the best intent in the world, cannot make a go of what has been called the most complicated and demanding of all human relationships.

The idea that there is only one person in the world for whom we are destined seems rather extreme. It is probably a hangover from childhood when one's mother may have seemed the whole world and no one else would do. A marriage based on the "one and only" belief often runs into difficulties, if not failure, because along with the feeling that the partner *is* the one and only goes the demand for perfection, just as the child usually expects his mother to be a goddess and above all human error.

It is the weak who are most likely to demand perfection. They look to the other person to be a Rock of Gibraltar against whom they can lean, trying to wear him down with a constant shower of weaknesses. The strong usually know the demand for perfection is an impossible one, that it has little to do with love. They are able to enjoy being mortal, with the capacity to accept feelings of both love and hate.

The emotionally mature person has a fairly serene existence. When life is seen through a veil of anger, even the good things may turn out poisonously. By the same token, unhappiness loses much of its intensity when life is felt as fairly quiet and smooth.

Respect for the other is a very important essential of marriage, not the kind of respect demanded by parents of children just because they are the parents, but a respect founded on admiration and liking. The person who feels respected by the mate is apt to be much happier in the marriage. If you feel a mate admires and enjoys, rather than envies and destroys, and is pleased by your achievements, not threatened or jealous of them, you will respond in like fashion.

The one who is emotionally mature usually respects himself, having made peace with himself. He is able to live in reasonable comfort and contentment. He does not expect the impossible from himself or the one he loves.

He accepts the reality of being human.

SUGGESTED READING

ACKERMAN, N. W., M.D. *The Psychodynamics of Family Life: Its Diagnosis and Treatment.* New York: Basic Books, Inc., 1958.

ENGLISH, O. SPURGEON, M.D. and CONSTANCE J. FOSTER. *Fathers Are Parents Too.* New York: G. P. Putnam's Sons, 1951.

———— and GERALD H. J. PEARSON, M.D. *Emotional Problems of Living.* New York: W. W. Norton & Company, Inc., 1945.

DANIELS, ANNA K. *The Mature Woman: Her Richest Years.* New York: Prentice-Hall, Inc., 1953.

DEUTSCH, HELENE H., M.D. *The Psychology of Women.* New York: Grune & Stratton, Inc., 1944.

FROMM, ERICH, Ph.D. *The Art of Loving.* New York: Harper & Brothers, 1956.

GLASSER, WILLIAM, M.D. *Mental Health or Mental Illness.* New York: Harper & Brothers, 1960.

GROTJAHN, MARTIN, M.D. *Psychoanalysis and the Family Neurosis.* New York: W. W. Norton & Company, Inc., 1960.

LEVY, JOHN and RUTH MUNROE. *The Happy Family.* New York: Alfred A. Knopf, Inc., 1938.

MEAD, MARGARET. *Male and Female.* New York: William Morrow & Co., Inc., 1949.

MUDD, EMILY H. and ARON KIRCH. *Man and Wife.* New York: W. W. Norton & Company, Inc., 1957.

POLATIN, PHILLIP and ELLEN C. PHILTINE. *The Well-adjusted Personality.* Philadelphia: J. B. Lippincott Co., 1952.

SPOCK, BENJAMIN, M.D. *Pocketbook of Baby and Child Care.* New York: Pocket Books, Inc., 1946.

STEVENSON, GEORGE S., M.D. *Mental Health Planning for Social Action.* New York: Blakiston Division, McGraw-Hill Book Co., 1956.

STONE, ABRAHAM, M.D. and HANNAH. *A Marriage Manual.* New York: Simon and Schuster, Inc., 1952.

VAN DE VELDE, TH. H. *Ideal Marriage.* New York: Random House, 1930.

Public Affairs Pamphlets

(Available at Public Affairs Office, 22 E. 38, New York City)

APPLEBAUM, STELLA G. *Working Wives and Mothers.*

BARUCH, DOROTHY, M.D. *How to Discipline Children.*

DUVALL, EVELYN and SYLVANUS. *Saving Your Marriage.*

ECKERT, RALPH G. *So You Think It's Love.*

OGG, ELIZABETH. *Why Some Women Stay Single.*

OSBORNE, ERNEST. *Democracy Begins in the Home.*

INDEX

Biographical Note

Lucy Freeman is the author of eight other books, including *The Story of Psychoanalysis,* written with Marvin Small. Her first book, *Fight Against Fears,* appeared in 1951 and was a best seller. Born in New York City, she attended Bennington College and soon after graduation began working for *The New York Times,* remaining there until she left to free lance in 1952. During her last six years at the *Times* she specialized in covering news in psychoanalysis, psychiatry, and social welfare. She was given the New York Newspaper Women's Award for the best news story of 1948, on the Texas City fire, and the first award of the New York Chapter of Theta Sigma Phi, national professional society for women journalists, in 1950, for "outstanding achievement in the newspaper field."

Harold Greenwald attended high school in Brooklyn, and got his bachelor's degree from CCNY and his master's and Ph.D. from Columbia. He is now engaged in the practice of individual and group psychoanalysis in New York City. He is also a lecturer in the Home and Family Life Department at Teachers College, Columbia University, consultant psychologist at Stuyvesant Polyclinic Hospital, and a member of the faculty of the training institute, National Psychological Association for Psychoanalysis. Past president of the Association for Applied Psychoanalysis, he is a member of the American Psychological Association, American Group Psychotherapy Association, National Psychological Association for Psychoanalysis, and other professional groups, and on the Executive Board of the Council of Psychoanalytic Psychotherapy.